CW00375808

POCKET FULL OF LEAVES

Patricia Denio

MINERVA PRESS

LONDON
MIAMI DELHI SYDNEY

POCKET FULL OF LEAVES
Copyright © Patricia Denio 2000

All Rights Reserved

No part of this book may be reproduced in any form
by photocopying or by any electronic or mechanical means,
including information storage or retrieval systems,
without permission in writing from both the copyright
owner and the publisher of this book.

ISBN 0 75411 047 8

First Published 2000 by
MINERVA PRESS
315–317 Regent Street
London W1R 7YB

Printed in Great Britain for Minerva Press

POCKET FULL OF LEAVES

Chapter One

It was the third of September, 1945; I shall never forget that day. I was eleven years old at the time and lived in a town called Warrington, Lancashire, England. The time was approximately 11 a.m. I had just finished bathing and dressing for the day so I decided to go and call on my cousin Doreen who lived across the street with my grandma and grandpa; their names were Lillian and Alfred.

I stepped out of my front door and what I was about to see was a very memorable experience. People were wonderfully happy – they were celebrating the end of World War Two. They sipped glasses of champagne and I had never seen so much beer. The women were bringing out food to put on tables that had been brought earlier and placed on a patch of land at the side of our house. It was land that had air-raid shelters where we had spent many, many nights.

I knocked on my grandma's door and Doreen answered. She came out and we walked up and down the street watching all the people. Then we walked to the air-raid shelter and sat on the steps leading down to the inside. We talked about the previous years when we would be asleep in our beds and the air-raid sirens would go off to alert us that enemy planes had been sighted.

My brother Rob and I shared a bedroom on the second floor of a beautiful, large old home on Golborne Street. We had twin beds and at the foot of each bed was a neatly folded Scottish plaid blanket ready to be wrapped around us as we were led by our parents into the air-raid shelters around the corner. We would sit along one side with our backs against the shelter wall, facing the row of neighbours sitting opposite us. The women would be knitting and sewing in the dim candlelight while the men would read their newspapers or talk quietly. Sometimes there would be silence in the shelter as we heard noises in the distance. We knew these could be bombs.

One morning after hearing the all-clear sirens, we left the shelter to return to our homes. One of the windows in our kitchen was broken. My mum found a piece of shrapnel on the ground outside and we guessed this had broken the window.

We found out a little later in the day that the town of Liverpool, just eighteen miles away, had been heavily bombed. We were so lucky in Warrington as it was only bombed on one occasion.

★

I cannot remember the date, but it happened on a Saturday afternoon. My granddad worked at a large paper mill and he had bought two tickets for my brother Rob and I to attend a big family picnic that was to be held at the mill. It was for families and relatives of all the people who worked there. My granddad gave the tickets to my mother, but due to a terrible argument she had had with my father the day of the picnic, she never took Rob and I. The mill was bombed sometime that afternoon and over 200 people were killed – once again how lucky Rob and I had been!

However, my granddad was badly injured and I can still see him laying there on the couch with bandages about ten inches deep, wrapped around his waist and stomach. He did survive and lived for many years afterwards.

There used to be men who would walk down the streets at night, checking every home to make sure there wasn't the least bit of light coming from anyone's windows, They would tap on the front door to let you know if there was. We always seemed to have had a problem in Rob's and my bedroom. My dad couldn't seem to block out all the light so my mother decided one night to wrap a piece of soft leather loosely around the small gas light that hung from the ceiling in our room. It was an unusual light and it reminded me of a soft eggshell as it was actually shaped like an egg. You had to hold a match to it as you turned a small, key-like object and this would turn the gas on. The night my mum wrapped the leather around the light to dim it, I woke up at about 2.30 a.m. We would have suffocated because the leather had started to smoulder from the heat and the room was thick with smoke. I banged on the wall to wake my dad and he rushed into our room, turned off the light and opened all the windows. It felt good to breathe fresh air again.

Rationing was something else we all had to cope with. We were each issued a ration book and were only allowed so much tea and bread or maybe I should just say that everything was rationed – even candy. We always had a good Sunday dinner, but the rest of the week we would live on cornflakes or bread and jam. If we were lucky, sometimes we would have fish and chips which was a luxury. I now look back and remind myself how fortunate are all those who survive a world war, or any war for that matter, but it did finally end and it was time for us all to move forward.

Maybe if my brother and I had had a happier home life it would have made things a little easier. Our parents had not got along for as long as we could remember; the bitter fights would keep us awake at night. Unfortunately they both had vicious tempers. Rob and I would lie in bed terrified at the terrible noises as they took turns at smashing all the furniture, including our beautiful china cabinet that was pushed completely over; breaking all its fragile contents. We would go downstairs in the morning to find blood on the walls from fighting and rubble from broken furniture or anything else they could put their hands on.

My parents had worked hard to put our home together. My dad had worked for the railway for many years. They never seemed to have had any money and had to buy furniture and such things on credit. They paid a few shillings a week which took years to pay off – how foolish they were to let their tempers flare so out of control. We had one of the loveliest homes in Warrington, even if we were poor.

One way we managed to save on money was the fact that my dad was very gifted. He had taught himself how to wallpaper the walls beautifully and he was an excellent electrician and plumber. I don't think there was anything he couldn't do. My mother was the one with the ideas; she knew how to make a home beautiful. The two of them together could make a place into a palace. I always thought this was unusual for my mother since she had been brought up in a terribly unhappy home herself. She had lost three beautiful little sisters when she herself was still a child. The first one died in my grandmother's arms when she had been very ill with a high fever.

The second one was killed while being taken for a walk in her baby carriage. A fourteen-year-old neighbour girl used to drop by and ask grandma if she could take the baby for a walk. One day the baby carriage tipped over when the girl had tried to get it off the sidewalk. The baby fell from the carriage and hit her head on the street. She died instantly.

Then there was beautiful Minnie, whose picture I have treasured to this day. She died in an ambulance on the way to the hospital after being diagnosed as having diphtheria. She was seven years old when she died.

All of this broke my grandmother's heart. She had a severe nervous breakdown and just seemed to have given up on life. She had kept a lovely home but drifted into becoming a bag lady. She would walk the streets, picking up bottles or anything she could find to turn into a few pennies. At 9.30 p.m. she would take her old white jug down to the corner pub and ask for a pint of beer which she would take home and have by the small fire she made from sticks she had found near the park. This seemed to be her only pleasure in life.

My granddad seemed to have given up also. He would sit in his old wicker chair all day and at night he would walk up the dark and creaking stairway carrying a candle. Then he would fall asleep on a grubby mattress which lay on an old brass bed.

My grandparents had raised my cousin Doreen since she was just a few days old. Her mother had four other children born before Doreen and she felt it was too much for her to care for and support all of the children. Another heartbreaking episode in my grandmother's life came when Doreen's mother came to take her back the day after she finished school, at the age of fifteen. She was now ready to go to work and help her parents.

My mother, Beatrice, was a very strong woman in one sense. She reminded me so much of Joan Crawford in the movie, *Mummy Dearest*. She was a domineering and vicious-tempered woman. I believe I understand why she was that way; probably most of it was due to her terrible home life when she was a child. The fights she and my father had, led her into another sad home situation. She had caught him with other women, which caused her to have two severe nervous breakdowns.

Chapter Two

During Christmas of 1942, after putting the house back together as best they could after one of their fights, my parents decided to have a party for a few of our close friends. Before the party started, they thought they would walk to the corner pub for a drink to celebrate the holidays. They left Rob and I at home and gave us colouring books and crayons. Mum asked us to sit and colour pictures until they came home. Rob and I were surprised to see them return that evening, bringing with them three American servicemen who were stationed at a nearby air force base. They were delighted to spend Christmas Eve in a nice, cosy home with a fire in the fireplace. My parents were in one of their good moods during that time. My dad played the piano. We sang and danced and had a wonderful time and of course I just had to do a little tap-dancing; something I loved to do when I was a young girl. All through my years of growing up, dancing was something I loved to do. I always wished I had continued tap and ballet.

My tap-dancing days had come to an abrupt halt at the age of eight. It happened one night upon returning home from a small community club that my mum and dad used to go to occasionally. During the afternoon of that day, my mum came into the parlour and decided to fix herself a cup of tea. She had been working in the wash house across the yard. Washing machines were unheard of in those days and she washed everything by hand in a large tub, then pushed everything through a wringer machine before hanging it all on a clothes line. As she came into the parlour, she found me making up my own little tap-dance routine. She asked to see it again, so I repeated the same steps. She then proceeded to tell me that she would take me to the community club dance that night.

She dressed me in the lovely little red and gold outfit that she and my dad had made for me. My dad had put glue on my tap shoes and then sprinkled gold glitter all over them. It was a beautiful costume. She then put my nice new necklace around my neck and a matching bracelet around my wrist; my friend had given them to me a few days before for my birthday.

That evening we had been at the dance for about two hours when mum asked the band to play a certain tune for me to dance to. I lost my nerve when I thought that maybe I wouldn't remember my new routine; I told her I didn't want to dance and she did the one thing I was afraid of – she went into a horribly bad mood – I could tell by her face.

It was about 12.30 a.m. when we returned home and she let all her anger out and smacked me, then grabbed the necklace from my neck and my bracelet. The beads scattered everywhere. Then she sent me up to bed and I lay there, too upset to even cry. I didn't want to tap-dance any more.

I lay thinking of the many places and parties I had danced at. On one occasion I was invited to dance at Peter Cane's wedding. He was a well-known boxer in England. As I came out from the side curtain, I slipped as my feet went from under me. People told my mum how they would always remember my big eyes as I looked up at the crowd with dismay showing on my face. Peter Cane came over to me and helped me back on my feet, dusted me off and asked me to continue on with my dance. During the curtsey at the end I received a standing ovation.

During the following days, which led into weeks after the Christmas party, one of the American servicemen named Steve, visited our home frequently. As the weeks turned into months there were more fights between my parents until finally my dad left our home and went to stay at his mother's, Steve began taking my mother out to dinner and dancing; he was very good to us – he brought us all kinds of gifts and candy. My dad would stop by to see us once in a while, but it was obvious that the marriage was over.

★

One day, some time in 1944, I was walking down the street with my mum and her only surviving sister, my Aunt Joyce. I heard my mum say to her that she hadn't told anyone she was expecting Steve's baby, which was due in September. My mum didn't realise that I had heard her say this and it was forty years later when she confided in me and told me who my sister's father was. I kept her secret and didn't tell her that I knew this all along.

The year 1944 was an awful year for my mum. Steve's tour of duty in England was coming to an end and he had to return to the U.S. He did promise mum that he would send for her as soon as his divorce became final. He had been honest with my mother from the beginning about having a wife back home but I don't know what really happened. We never heard from him again.

September came and mum gave birth to a beautiful daughter. She named her Helen. Her little face was like a peach, so round and soft and she had lovely blue eyes and blonde hair. How sad it was that Steve never knew her.

The months ahead were extremely hard for my mother, now she had the three of us to care for. There was one thing that would keep us going – each of us had a great sense of humour. My mum would always end up being the life of a party and we had so many good laughs together in spite of all the pitfalls.

It was during that time when my mother took a job driving a bread van, delivering bread and pastries to various small grocery stores. She had a helper with her named Ken, who was a character. Ken stood about five feet two inches and wore thick horn-rimmed spectacles. One day when they were out making deliveries, they came out from one of the grocery stores and found that the van wouldn't start. They checked under the bonnet and just about everywhere they could think of.

At that point my mum said to Ken, 'I think we may be out of petrol.' (The petrol gauge never did work right.)

He looked up at her over his glasses and said, 'Mrs Robertson, I know how we can tell if we are out of petrol.'

She asked, 'How do we do that, Ken?'

His reply was, 'If you drop a pebble in the tank and it splashes, that means it's not empty, but if we hear it hit the bottom, then we are in trouble.' Mum just looked at him and shook her head as if to say, I don't believe you said that, Ken. Finally help came along and they managed to get it started.

On another occasion during the time when bread was heavily rationed, the van caught fire and destroyed all the bread. My mother panicked with fear at wondering what would happen to her if she was caught with all of the wasted bread. Well, Ken came up with another brainwave. The next thing they did was drive whatever was left of the van back to our house. They took three hours to scoop all the water out of our beautiful little duck pond which my dad had built a couple of years before. They tossed all the burnt bread into the empty duck pond, then covered it over with soil. I shall never forget my dad's face when he came to visit Rob and I soon after that, as he looked through the window to find his pond had completely vanished. We had a lot of laughs as we looked back on that.

Chapter Three

During the year 1946, my mum went over to the house of a neighbour who was also a good friend of hers. They had a cup of tea together and while my mother was there, another of the neighbour's friends stopped by and was introduced to mum. His name was Paul. I gather that it must have been love at first sight because he started to drop by the neighbour's more frequently, hoping to see my mum there. One day she was there and he asked to take her to the movies. She accepted and they started seeing each other every night.

Paul and my mother went together steady after that. He wanted to marry her, but she wasn't ready for marriage yet. She hadn't got over Steve and she was determined to see him again somehow, some way.

★

November of 1947, Paul was given a Christmas bonus from the company he had worked for, for seventeen years. He came to the house one afternoon on his way home from work and he gave the bonus money to mum to put away for us to all have a nice Christmas with. I shall never forget what she did with the money. She immediately got a passport and a plane ticket to Canada. I know she was really making her way to the States to see Steve. She waited until one night after dark and had Rob and I wait in the back yard. Her suitcases were placed in a baby carriage and we were instructed to wait there and peep through the window into the living room. The minute we saw Paul arrive we had to leave through the back way and push the baby carriage with her luggage in it to the train station. She waited twenty minutes, then told Paul that she was going to look for us as we were out playing with our friends in the neighbourhood. Paul waited at the house, believing her. She finally arrived at the train station and boarded for Southampton. Rob and I then took the baby carriage home. We put it in the back yard, then went around to the front door and walked in. We asked Paul where Mum was and he said she was out looking for us. We felt bad for Paul – he was such a great guy.

Rob and I were told to say nothing about my mother leaving the way she did. She also told us to go to bed and to get up the following morning and go to school. When school let out at 4 p.m. we were to go to my grandma's house where my dad was staying and wait for him to come home from work. This we did.

We had to ask Dad to come to our house and take care of us because Mum had gone on a short vacation and would be back home soon. We were to tell him that we didn't know where she had decided to go.

My dad was angry but had no alternative and he came home with us. In the meantime Paul was frantic and contacted the Police Department. Two days later he talked to my dad and was told she had gone on a short vacation. Paul then got suspicious and thought of Steve in the States. He took a bus to Liverpool and visited the Immigration Department. They had no one listed by the name of Beatrice Robertson as leaving for America. He didn't even think of her going to Canada. My mother had been gone about eight days when we received a letter from her. She admitted to my dad that she was in Canada. Rob and I never told anyone that we knew where she was.

In the letter she told my dad not to spoil anything for her or do anything to cause her to have to come back. She said she was happy in Canada and had a good job at a country club. She also told Dad that she would be sending for Rob, Helen and me as soon as she got her feet on the ground. My dad was furious. He told all of this to Paul, but Paul felt there was nothing he could do at this point and could only wait and see what happened.

I was now thirteen years old and I guess you might say I was the lady of the house. I tried to keep everything in the home the way my mum had done. On Saturday mornings I would clean the whole house from top to bottom and Sundays I would be in the wash house, washing all the clothes, sheets and blankets as well.

We still had to wash by hand.

Rob and I would place two step ladders side-by-side so we could both reach the clothes line. He had to go one step higher since he was shorter than me. I dreaded having him to help me hang the blankets.

One day I was so angry I saw red. With Rob's help I had washed and hung four blankets on the line but the weight of them broke the line and they all fell to the ground. I had to wash them all again.

Chapter Four

The fifth of November, Guy Fawkes Night; the night that they build bonfires all over England. In the weeks before bonfire night, kids all over the country would collect wood from anywhere they could find it, and each bunch of kids would have their own storing place.

During the day of this particular bonfire night, a couple of men stationed at an army base parked their big army truck on the same patch of land where the air-raid shelters were. This is where we were having our bonfire and they were watching all the kids stack the wood up ready to light that night. The two soldiers decided to help us kids out, so they drove away in the truck and about four hours later they returned with the truck almost full of wood. They stacked it on top of what was already there and the kids were delighted, saying how ours was going to be the best bonfire in England. The kids never had a chance to enjoy it – the night turned into a horror scene. Just before the fire was lit, one of the army men decided it would light better if he threw some gasoline on the wood. The other army man put a big, rolled up piece of newspaper which he lit on the end to start the fire. All of a sudden, flames shot out from everywhere. I will always remember the screams as kids ran in all directions. I saw Rob run by me toward home. I ran after him and saw that he was red from his face down to his ankles (the English lads used to wear the short trousers which didn't help in this particular incident).

My dad wrapped a large bath towel around Rob and sat him on the handlebars of his bicycle, then rushed him to the hospital which was two miles away. Thank God his burns were not severe, like many of the other kids' were. He was treated and released, but really suffered for a couple of weeks.

There were ambulances at the scene of the fire. The worst accident was the soldier who had lit the fire – his hand was so burnt he had to have it amputated.

During this time we had another problem which we had to deal with. It was what we were going to do with Helen while Rob and I were in school and Dad was at work. The lady that used to take care of her had moved to a new location so I had to take a couple of weeks off school to take care of her. During the second week, my dad managed to find a day nursery for babies ranging in age between six months and five years, after which age they started school. It was difficult for me during the time that Helen was in the nursery. It meant that I had to catch two buses in the morning; one went in one direction to the nursery and then one from the nursery to school which was on the other side of town. It was a repeat at 4 p.m. when I got out of school. Helen and I would finally arrive home at about 5.15 p.m.

One day after Helen had been at the nursery for about three months, I went to pick her up as usual after school. When I arrived, the nurse told me that Helen wasn't feeling good. I thought that maybe she was coming down with a cold, so I took her home and laid her on the couch with a blanket over her.

The next day she didn't look good at all, so I kept her home and tried to get a little food down her, such as canned peaches or pears. She ate very little and looked awfully drawn and pale. Finally, on the fourth day I waited for Rob to come home from school and as soon as he arrived I sent him to bring Aunt Joyce. She came back with him on the next bus. Aunt Joyce started to cry when she saw Helen but she also got angry and started to say what she thought of my mum for leaving us like she did. She dressed Helen in some warm clothes and took her home with her. She immediately called the doctor who was at Aunt Joyce's within the hour. The doctor was shocked to see how sick Helen was and had her taken to the hospital right away. Aunt Joyce was told that Helen had meningitis and would have died, probably within the next three days. Thank God, she was being cared for and gradually started to show signs of improvement. She was in the hospital for about a month, until she was allowed to go home with Aunt Joyce. She still needed to be cared for with plenty of rest until she regained her strength.

Two weeks after Helen was released from the hospital, I had just left home to go to school when I heard someone call my name. I looked across the street and was shocked to see my mother standing in grandma's doorway. She called for me to go over, which I did. We both went into grandma's house and once we were inside she flew into a rage and proceeded to beat me all through the living room. She was screaming at me, asking me why I hadn't told her about Helen and Rob.

I tried to explain that I didn't want to worry her and that I had been doing the best I could for Helen and she was all right now, and that Rob was also doing fine, I believe it was my granddad who had written and told her everything. My mum finally calmed down and then told me to go back home and pack some clothes in a bag. She said she was taking me to Aunt Joyce's with her. I left and walked back across the street to my home. I just didn't know what Dad was going to do. The first thing I did was write him a note, explaining what had happened and I left it on the kitchen table. I then proceeded to pack some clothes in a paper bag. After I finished, I checked around the house to make sure that everything was neat, then walked back over to my grandma's house.

My mother and I walked down the street and caught the bus to Aunt Joyce's house. When we arrived, my aunt didn't look too happy about the whole situation, but she told us to make ourselves comfortable and fixed us a cup of tea. We spent most of the day just sitting and talking. Then Mum and Aunt Joyce started to prepare dinner for when Uncle Charlie came home from work.

My uncle had to go over to his sister's house that evening to fix a broken water pipe in the bathroom. He had only been gone a little while when we heard a knock on the front door. My aunt went to answer it and found that it was my dad standing there. He asked if my mum and I would step outside as he wanted to talk to us. My mother and I walked down the street with him as he had to catch a bus back home. All the way down the street my parents were arguing. He let one bus go by and still they continued to argue. My dad asked Mum why she had come back from Canada without letting anyone know and what right had she to come and take me away like she did. My mother yelled at him and said she should have been told of Helen's illness and Rob's accident and that she needed me to take care of Helen. When the bus came toward us my dad grabbed my arm and started to pull me toward the bus. My mother had hold of my other arm and screamed, saying that I was going with her. As my dad boarded the bus, he let go of my arm.

I felt so terrible. For the first time in my life I wanted to be away from everyone and everything. I was wishing I could be in a little room somewhere, sitting in a rocking chair and listening to some nice quiet music all by myself. Instead I walked back to my aunt's house and went upstairs to bed.

Chapter Five

The next two weeks were hectic. Mum and I walked all over town looking for a place to rent. We finally found a room at the back of an elderly couple's home. They let us have the bedroom upstairs and my mum, Helen, and I moved in and made it as comfortable as possible.

We stayed at this home for two months while waiting for our names to come up on a waiting list for a new house, which finally came along. It was in an estate on the other side of town.

Just before we moved into our new house, my mum and Paul were married. Paul was a wonderful man and forgave my mum for everything she had done. I was proud to have him as my stepfather. They had been married for eighteen months when my mum had another baby daughter, whom they named Kathleen. She was as beautiful as Helen.

Times seemed happier now. We loved our new home but there was one particular evening I always remember. I thought that for sure my mother would kill me this time. She and Paul had to walk to the store to pick up a few groceries. Just before they left, my mother placed a large family-sized can of peas in a pan of boiling water that she left on a low light to keep hot. She told me to leave it on for fifteen minutes, then turn the stove off.

I waited until they left and then went into the living room to play the piano. I couldn't read music, but I used to fantasise that I was a great pianist. I got carried away trying to play the *Warsaw Concerto*, when I suddenly heard a massive explosion, I was trembling as I slowly walked through the house to see what it could be when, finally, I entered the kitchen. I couldn't believe my eyes, the whole place was green – Mum had forgotten to puncture the can of peas. I nearly died while trying to clean up the mess. The pan had flown all the way through the front hall and hit the front door. The stove was also damaged. If there was ever a time I felt like running away from home, it was then. Thank God

Mum was forgiving when she realised that she had forgotten to puncture the can of peas.

During those months of moving and everything that happened, my mum kept me home from school repeatedly. My education was atrocious. Whenever they sent someone from the School Board to see why I wasn't attending school, Mum always had an excuse ready. She would say I was sick or another time she told them that I was attending a school in another town (which I wasn't). I don't believe the school authorities ever checked to see if I was in another school because nothing was ever done about it. Kids in those days finished school at the age of fifteen and I believe I only went to school half of the years that I should have been going.

It was approximately one week after my fourteenth birthday that my mum found me a job as a waitress in a café. I went there right after school and worked the evening shift. I gave Mum my pay cheque and she would let me keep a little of my tip money. I would take two shillings and put it away so I could go dancing on a Saturday night. I lived all week for that. The rest I would try to save or buy a new top or pair of shoes with it.

★

My fifteenth birthday finally arrived. I was so happy to leave school as I had grown to hate the times I would be there. The kids in my class used to whisper behind my back and say how dumb I was. I have to admit that I was really behind in school due to all the absenteeism.

I continued on with the café job, but found another job during the day working in a stationery store. I loved the two girls I worked with and we became lifelong friends. We all used to go to the same dance hall on a Saturday night, then they would come home with me and stay the night rather than leave the dance early in order to catch the last bus home.

Chapter Six

When I was seventeen I met my first love. He lived on the same new estate as I did and we both got off the bus one particular evening and struck up a conversation as we walked from the bus stop to our homes. We started seeing each other after that and I really fell in love with him. His name was Tim. Two of the things we enjoyed doing the most were going to the movies and I loved to watch him run. He was very athletic and ran in many races. He had lots of medals and trophies and I always felt so proud of him.

Tim and I went together for about eight months. Then one evening as I stepped off the bus on my way home from work his mother was there to meet me. She had tears in her eyes as she proceeded to tell me that my mum had been to see her that day and told her that she didn't want Tim to see me any more. Mum had said that I was too young to go steady and that I should date other boys. I was heartbroken; I just could not believe that she could do this to me. Tim came to see me at work the next day. He wondered if we should just take off, but we were so afraid. That was the last time I saw Tim.

The evenings were long and lonely after the break-up. I knew it was no use to try and see Tim as my mother would have caught me. Even on the Saturday nights when I used to go dancing with my girlfriends, my mother would come to the dance hall and watch me for a while. She was probably checking to see if I was leaving with a boy. She had given me a strict upbringing and said I should save myself for marriage though I had never once gone to bed with anyone.

During the time I was seeing Tim I had given up my evening job, but now I needed something to do to rid me of the loneli-ness. I decided to look in the newspaper for some kind of job I could do in the evening. I came across an ad by an American family stationed at the same base where Steve had been. I wrote to them immediately and to my surprise the husband came to see me and told me they would be happy for me to babysit their three children. Little did I know that that ad would change my whole future.

I started my new babysitting job the following weekend and it led into three or four evenings a week. The children were beautiful. The oldest one was David, who was eight years old, Barbara was five and Mary was just three months old. She was a doll and such a good baby. The parents' names were John and Jenny McIntyre. I continued to work for them for the following year, then one day Mr Mc sent for my mother. They had a long talk and he told her that his tour of duty in England was coming to an end and that he and his family would soon be returning to the States. He asked my mother if she would consider letting me follow them. It would be impossible to leave at the same time since I would have a lot of paperwork to do in order to get a passport and it also meant a trip to Liverpool for a physical.

My mother came home that evening and discussed all of this with me. She told me that the McIntyres would sponsor me and pay my fare to the States. I was overjoyed at the thought of going to America – it was a dream come true. I asked Mum how she would feel about me leaving. Her answer was that she thought I could do much better with my life in the States and that there were much more opportunities there than there were in England. So the decision was made. I would leave for America as soon as possible.

The McIntyres left for the States in August, 1952. I finally received my passport and was able to buy a few new clothes to take with me. Mr Mc sent me a ticket to sail on a ship called the *Ascania*.

I left for the States on 22 December,1952. I was eighteen years old. My mother and Paul came to see me off and I will always remember waving to them as we pulled out of the harbour in Liverpool. I had tears in my eyes as I went further and further away. I thought of my sisters and Rob, also of my wonderful girlfriends whom I was leaving behind, but the next thing I felt was a surge of excitement as I thought of my new life in America. Finally I left the deck and went to the cabin that I shared with three other women. The next thing we had to do after our introductions was to change our clothes and freshen up, then go to the dining room. I was placed at a table with a young couple whose names were Jean and Roy; they were heading to California for a six-week vacation. Also at our table was another girl about the same age as myself. Her name was Celia. She was from Ireland and was emigrating to the States. Her destination was Boston, Massachusetts.

My first day on board was wonderful. Celia and I instantly became friends and we were inseparable during the whole journey except for the days that I became terribly seasick and had to stay in bed. I could hardly move my head, I felt so awful. Finally on the fourth day the chief steward came and knocked on my cabin door. He said I must try to make it to the dining room and eat something. After a hard struggle of trying to get back on my feet, I took a shower and got dressed and made it to the dining room. I will always remember that meal. It was baked chicken that was good, but I had never had creamed-style corn in my life. I thought the smell of it was awful and it made me sick all over again. It took me all of the next thirty years to learn to like creamed-style corn.

Following my bout with seasickness, I started to feel really good again. Celia and I were together again so one day we decided to explore the ship. We ended up getting lost and found ourselves in the first class section. We joined in nicely and had tea at 4 p.m. in the fancy lounge area. They had a band playing soft music and all of a sudden we noticed that the men in the band were the same ones who had played the night before in our tourist section. The music they played for us was certainly different; for us they played real swinging music. They spotted Celia and I sitting there and winked at us. We sat there grinning back at them.

We had a wonderful time on the ship even if I did sleep with my feet pushed through one of the small lifebelts that everyone was provided with. I figured that if anything happened and we started to sink, I would reach down and quickly pull up the lifebelt around my waist. I guess there is nothing like being ten steps ahead.

We had spent eleven days on board when someone got the word around that New York could be seen and everyone rushed on deck. What a fabulous sight! It was evening and all the lights were on. It reminded me of a wonderful fairyland, We stood looking at it for two or three hours as it was a wonderful sight, plus we had spent Christmas and New Year on the ship which made it all the more wonderful and exciting.

We pulled into the harbour at approximately 1 p.m. the next afternoon. Just before disembarking, an alarm went off in my overnight bag. It was very embarrassing when a couple of men came and checked out my bags. They must have thought I was carrying a bomb. We found it was nothing more than my alarm clock and I always believed it must have been one of the women in my cabin that set it to go off at that time. People that had gathered to watch had been told to stand back, but all had a good laugh, including myself.

Once on the ground, I said my goodbyes to Celia. We promised to correspond with each other and the young couple and I headed for the Greyhound bus terminal. We each bought our tickets and decided to leave that evening so that we could have a few hours to look around New York.

We found ourselves walking down this one particularly busy street. When we came to a jewellery store, we could hear an auctioneer inside so we decided to go in to see what it was all about. It was inexpensive jewellery but quite nice. There were hundreds of necklaces and bracelets and the store started to get crowded with people.

I thought it was odd that it was my first day in America and I had only just arrived a couple of hours before when I had my first unusual experience. I was standing with the couple, surrounded by people, when I suddenly felt someone tap me on the back of my shoulder. I turned to see a man who smiled at me and asked if I would just step into a side room as someone there wished to speak with me. I couldn't understand this as I didn't know a soul in New York. The couple looked at me questioningly and I asked them to wait there for me while I saw what it was all about.

I followed the stranger into the room and sitting at a desk was a heavy-set man, puffing on a cigar. He wore a suit and I noticed a diamond pin in his tie. He must have been able to tell by my clothes that I certainly wasn't from New York. I had on an Irish tweed suit with fur-lined boots, plus a beret on my head. The first thing he asked me was where I was heading and I told him I was on my way to Texas. He then proceeded to tell me that I wouldn't like it there, that it was just a desert and too hot. I told him that I had people waiting for me but he told me to send them a telegram to say I had changed my mind and he said he would pay for it. This man went on to say that he would put me up in a hotel and pay all expenses. Also he said he would show me all around New York and give me anything I needed. At this point, as naive as I was, I figured he was looking for girls to be prostitutes to work for him. I got a little nervous but kept my cool, I told him I would think about it and would return in an hour to let him know my decision.

I guess he must have believed me because he said he would be waiting. I left his office and went to join the couple who was waiting there for me in the store. I stood there for a while; I did not want to look too anxious to leave in case the man was still watching me. After a few minutes went by I whispered to the couple that I thought we should leave, so we walked out of the store. Once outside I told them what had happened and we did a really fast disappearing act.

We walked around for approximately an hour and a half, then decided to go to the afternoon movie. We bought our tickets and went inside and sat down. To our surprise, all of a sudden the lights went down and the curtains opened. Instead of a movie it turned out to be a real live onstage Burlesque show. We just couldn't help but laugh at how our first day in the States was turning out.

We left the show and decided to go and have a snack, then from there we headed for the Greyhound bus station. We all agreed that we had enjoyed our crazy afternoon in New York. We were amazed at all the high buildings and found it to be fun watching the different characters walk along the streets.

Finally we reached the bus terminal and had tears in our eyes as we wished each other good luck and goodbye. The young couple then boarded their bus and waved to me as it drove away.

I stood there waiting for my bus and was delighted to see another couple come walking to the bus stop. They had also been on the same ship coming from England. We shook hands and then found we were to get on the same bus at least for part of the way. We boarded the bus and the couple sat on the seat directly behind me. We chatted for quite a while and talked about our day in New York. It was so relaxing to sit down and rest. It started to get late and people started to doze off.

Chapter Seven

It was approximately 5.30 a.m. when the driver pulled into a rest stop and told us we all had a ten-minute break. We strolled into the restaurant and I sat with the couple. I ordered coffee and they both asked for a cup of tea. It took a few minutes to get served due to all the other people from the bus.

We finally got our coffee and tea and the couple looked at their tea bags floating in their cups of hot water. We had never seen tea bags before. That was something else we didn't have in England. I couldn't help but be amused when, just as the driver told us it was time to get back on the bus, the man next to me started to choke.

As his wife pounded him on the back, she turned to the driver and said, 'Half a mo, chum, he swallowed the bloody label.'

It took a couple of seconds to dislodge the tea bag from his throat, he was grumbling all the way back to the bus and said that he would never drink tea while on his visit to the States ever again.

We returned to our seats and took off once again. It was starting to get late and people started to doze off once again until finally it was daylight. It was great to see all the different sights along the way.

It was the next night when the couple departed from the bus and once again I found myself saying goodbye. I wondered if I would ever see any of these people from the ship ever again. So far it had been a wonderful trip.

Finally after two and a half days on the bus I reached my destination, a small town called San Marcos in between Austin and San Antonio. I gathered my suitcases and walked into the bus station. I called Mrs Mc and within ten minutes she was there to pick me up.

I shall never forget how she laughed as she drove towards me. She said she couldn't believe my outfit and that I should have been arriving at the North Pole rather than Texas. It was January, but I couldn't get over how hot it was.

We arrived at the house within minutes, and carried my luggage to what was to be my room. The house was beautiful. I found myself just walking around, looking through all the open doors into each room. I thought to myself how lucky I was to have the opportunity to stay in such a lovely home.

The first thing I did was to have a wonderful, refreshing shower and put on clean clothes. Then I walked into the kitchen where Mrs Mc had fixed us lunch. It was the first banana sandwich with mayonnaise that I had ever had and the coffee tasted out of this world.

We sat for a while during lunch as I talked about my trip and of the people I met along the way. She was sort of shocked when I told her about the man in the jewellery store in New York. She asked all about my family back in England.

Finally I started to clear the dishes off the table. As I wiped off the counter tops, she decided to call Mr Mc at the base to let him know I had arrived. He was delighted that I had the long trip over with and had no problems finding my way He said he would be home in the next hour to greet me, but could only stay a short while as he had to return to the base. Once Mrs Mc hung up the phone I turned towards her and to be polite, asked her if there was anything she would like me to do. I was a little surprised at her answer. I thought she may have told me to take it easy for the rest of the day since I had been travelling for two weeks, but instead she said she hadn't bothered to do very much around the house since she knew I would be there. The next I knew she was handing me the vacuum and dust rags.

Mr Mc arrived home within the hour of her calling him. He looked kind of startled to find me waxing the hardwood floors with paste wax which had to be polished afterwards. I guess he couldn't understand why she had me working already, but he never said anything to her.

I stood up and went to shake his hand but I thought I had better wash mine first. He smiled and said how happy they were that I was there and proceeded to tell me about all the work there was to be done around the house. I told him not to worry, that I would do my very best.

Mr Mc left the house and went back to the base. I then carried on cleaning. My intuition told me that I was in for some hard work, which I didn't mind, but I thought of the next three years, which was how long I had agreed to stay with them in return for their paying my boat fare. The ticket cost them $150 and three years looked like a long time, but I was here now so there wasn't anything I could do about it.

As I was cleaning the living room I noticed there were a lot of plants under the big bay window and a lot of dry leaves had fallen from them. Rather than go all the way back to the kitchen for the trash can, I gathered all the leaves up and stuffed them into my pockets. I figured I could get rid of them later, I then ran the vacuum and finished just in time to greet the two older kids as they came home from school. The baby had been sleeping the whole afternoon.

We all enjoyed a pleasant evening around the dinner table. Mrs Mc was a great cook which was the one thing she liked to do, although I would give her a hand peeling potatoes and washing the vegetables and so on.

It was now approximately 7.30 p.m. After cleaning up the kitchen and bathing the kids it was so relaxing to sit and watch a good movie on TV before finally going to bed around 11 p.m.

Chapter Eight

During the following several months, we would go for drives so that I could get used to where the stores and post office were. We would start off our Sundays by first going to church, something I had never done before. I made friends with many of the college kids there, but couldn't spend much time with them since the McIntyres only allowed me one night a week off.

San Marcos was a nice little town, although there wasn't much to do for a single person. It was a dry county, though that was unimportant to me since I had never drunk in my life. They used to have a dance once in a while and I did manage to go a couple of times, but Mrs Mc sort of frowned upon it since she was a born-again Christian and was a member of a strict Baptist Church. Mr Mc was not a member, but would go with the family.

I did enjoy swimming. Sometimes Mrs Mc would suggest taking an afternoon off so that we could go to the pool at the base. That's where I got my first terrible sunburn; coming from England I wasn't used to such hot sunshine. One of the other things I enjoyed was a short visit with the next-door neighbours, Charlene and Bill Radcliffe. Once in a while Charlene would come and ask Mrs Mc if she could take me to San Antonio shopping. I went twice, but couldn't buy very much since Mr Mc only paid me six dollars a week. I remember the second time that we went there and Charlene bought me a lovely pair of red, high-heeled shoes with a matching handbag. After shopping we went and had a late lunch. I was surprised when she started to ask me if I would consider moving in with her and her husband. She said she didn't like the way the McIntyres had me working so hard. She even offered to pay the McIntyres whatever it had cost them to bring me over.

I thanked Charlene as she was a good friend, but I told her I just couldn't do it since we lived next door. She also offered to send me to college to get the education that I had never had in my life. Maybe I was crazy not to take her up on it.

We enjoyed our day in San Antonio. I couldn't wait to wear my high-heeled shoes. I knew that once I wore them I would feel like a grown-up young lady instead of a teenage girl. I thanked Charlene again as she dropped me off at the house.

Chapter Nine

Finally, one whole year had gone by when one afternoon Mr Mc came home early. It was about 3 p.m. He said he would like to talk to me so we sat down at the kitchen table. He told me that one of the other Master Sergeants, named Larry, who was in his squadron, had bought a café on the outskirts of San Marcos and that he was looking for some good help to work there. Mr Mc asked me if I would like to work as a waitress for Larry. I was sort of startled by this. My first question was, who was going to do the housework? Mr Mc said that he had told Larry I could work at the café in the evenings so that I could do the housework during the day. Larry had told Mr Mc that he would pay me approximately $20 a week and that I probably would make that much in tips. Mr Mc then said that maybe I could split it with them towards my room and board. I couldn't believe all this, splitting with them and yet still doing all the housework and ironing! Anyway, I did decide to take the café job because I would at least be able to start saving for a trip back to England.

My job at the café started two weeks later. However, due to the other waitress who had a couple of kids and could only work certain hours, the schedule was changed. I worked Monday, Wednesday, Friday and Sunday from 4 p.m. until 11.30 p.m. Tuesday, Thursday and Saturday I worked from 11 a.m. until 7 p.m. This was a seven-day-a-week job.

I had plenty of time at home to do the housework and ironing, but looked forward every day to going to my café job. It was great to earn some extra money. Every Friday I would leave $15 on the piano for Mrs Mc and $5 I would spend on cab fare to work since I didn't have a car. The first thing I did was open a bank account and each week I would deposit my tips.

Most of the customers that came into the café were young servicemen from the base. They all knew that I loved earrings so whenever they made cross-country flights, (since most of them were pilots) they would bring me back a pair of earrings. I must have had hundreds of them. They came from Mexico and Nevada and many other places.

I remember one particular night when I was cleaning up the café before closing at about 10.45 p.m. There wasn't a soul in the place when this young man came in and sat at the counter. I could tell he had been drinking and he asked for a cup of coffee and a pizza pie. I had never heard of pizza pie and I thought he was asking for a piece of pie. I gave him his coffee, then pointed to the pie case.

I said, 'We have apple, cherry, coconut and lemon.'

He snapped at me and repeated, 'I want a pizza pie!'

I said, 'Yes, sir, I heard you the first time,' and once again showed him what we had in the pie case.

He then got more angry and said, 'A pizza pie! A pizza pie!'

I lost my temper and said, 'Well, that's all you get is a piece – you don't get the whole damn pie!'

At this point he put his head in his hands, then said in a more gentle voice, 'You know, a pizza pie with mushrooms on it?'

By now I was so aggravated I reached into the pie case, took out a piece of apple pie and walked into the kitchen. I asked the chef (he was a six-foot five-inch black guy who appeared to be seven feet with his chef's hat on) if he would please sprinkle a few mushrooms on top of the apple pie. His eyes went as big as saucers. He then picked up his meat cleaver and proceeded to chase me out of the kitchen.

He hollered, 'Don't you come ordering things like that at eleven o'clock at night!'

I leaped out of the kitchen, looked at the guy sitting there, threw up my hands and asked him if he would settle for a piece of cake. At that point he threw a quarter on the counter for his coffee and walked out. I stuck my tongue out at him as he went through the door and muttered to myself, 'Jerk!'

It was during the next afternoon when the boss and his wife dropped by the café that they asked me about the guy who had been there the night before. Evidently, Charlie (the chef) had mentioned something to them. I told them the whole story when they started to roar with laughter and then explained to me what the guy had been asking for. I then learned what pizza pie was.

Chapter Ten

The second year went by quickly with working so much. Then as I started into my third year with the McIntyres, I noticed that Mr Mc was working some strange hours. I never asked questions as I figured it was none of my business. Once he had come home from the base a little after 5 p.m. He had supper, washed and changed, then left again around 7 p.m. I took it for granted that he was going back to the base.

I did think it odd when he would be gone all night and he would come home around 7 a.m., go to bed, then return to the base at noon. This was going on three or four times a week. Finally, Mrs Mc told me that he was sort of running his own private taxi service, taking some of the servicemen to Austin or San Antonio so they could go to the clubs since there wasn't anything to do in San Marcos.

I told Mrs Mc it sounded like a pretty good idea, especially since the guys must have been paying him. I didn't think any more about it until one evening one of the young men from his squadron came in the café and he asked me if Mrs Mc knew what Mr Mc was doing when he was gone all night. I told him that she did know and that Mr Mc was just running some of the guys to different places. The young man looked at me and started to laugh. He told me that Mr Mc wasn't doing any such thing and that what he was really doing was gambling all night and that he had just lost $300 two nights before.

I couldn't believe it. All I could think about was how Mrs Mc would die if she knew the truth. I decided to stay out of it so I never said a word to Mrs Mc or anyone.

I didn't know that the second shock I had was going to be even worse. It was one particular morning when I had to go to work at 11 a.m. I always got up at the same time as Mrs Mc and the kids. Mr Mc came rolling in at the usual time, 7 a.m., and went to bed. Mrs Mc had to take the children to school that day and then she went on to the church where a bunch of the women were having some kind of a meeting. I did my usual chores around the house, such as washing the breakfast dishes and making the beds. I then went into the bathroom to start getting ready for work. As I was standing in the shower I nearly died with shock. The shower curtain slid open and Mr Mc was standing there looking at me and grinning. I screamed for him to get out and I threw the wash-cloth in his face, then grabbed the shower curtain and wrapped it around me. He walked out of the bathroom laughing to himself, as if it was all a joke. I could hardly finish getting ready, my knees were shaking so badly. I knew from that moment on it wouldn't be the same in that house again. Up until that point he had never once given me any indication that something like that would ever happen.

There had once been a small skeleton key that was used to lock the bathroom from the inside, but we figured that Mary may have taken it out of the keyhole and lost it somewhere. If the door was closed we all knew to knock first before entering.

I couldn't wait to get to work. I finished getting ready in a hurry, then dashed to the nearest pay phone to call a cab to take me to work. I knew I had to make a stop on the way; that was to the hardware store. I picked up a hook for the bathroom door.

I couldn't stop thinking about what had happened. It was hard to keep my mind on my work. I didn't tell a soul, not even my friend Marie with whom I worked – she too was a waitress.

That night when I arrived home from work, I put the hook on the inside of the bathroom door. I knew Mrs Mc would wonder what I was doing, so I just casually said to her that it was probably a good idea for when we had guests at the house who might feel uncomfortable if they couldn't lock the door. Thank goodness she went along with it.

I found it very uncomfortable to be in the house. I avoided Mr Mc as much as I could. I was thankful to see him leave again after supper, but dreaded the days that Mrs Mc might leave early again.

It wasn't until a month and a half later that the next episode happened. Once again it was on a morning when Mrs Mc had left early. I had just finished getting ready for work when he came walking out of the bedroom with just his undershorts on.

I went to reach for the doorknob to leave when all of a sudden he grabbed me and had me up against the wall. He was trying to kiss me as I was fighting him off. I was frantic as he started to get forceful; it was now becoming a drag out fight at that point. I yelled out that I was going to tell his wife and he suddenly stopped. At that point I made a dash for my bedroom and quickly locked the door from the inside. I stood and composed myself and wondered what to do for a minute. I knew there was only one way out and that was through the window which led out on to the front porch. I opened it wide then I knew I had to unlock the door before leaving in case Mrs Mc had to go into my room for any reason. I don't think I have ever climbed through a window so fast in my life. I ran the next three miles to Marie's house. I banged on the door and couldn't believe the look on her face as she asked me in. I knew at this point that I had to confide in someone, so I told Marie everything, including the attempted rape that had just occurred. She could not believe what I was telling her and she sort of sat in shock as she waited for me to come out of her bathroom where I was trying to straighten myself up. One of my earrings had fallen off during the scuffle, my hair was a mess, my stockings had runs in them and one of the pockets on my uniform was torn.

Marie let me use one of her bathrobes while she sewed my pocket back on. She had a cup of coffee sitting on the coffee table for us. As I sat down and reached for mine she looked at me questioningly, then asked me why I hadn't called the police.

I said, 'Marie, how could I?' I had Mrs Mc to think about and what would it do to their marriage, and what about the kids? Marie finally agreed that it was a hell of a predicament to be in.

Finally, we had to leave for the café. On the way there, Marie said that from that day on she would come by the house and wait for me while I got ready. I told her I would call her whenever Mrs Mc would leave early. I knew this was going to be a hardship for Marie because she didn't always work the same hours as myself.

I could hardly keep my mind on my work that afternoon as it was racing a million miles an hour! I wondered which was the best way to handle the situation. I was asking God to give me an answer and somehow I believed He would.

I finished work about 7 p.m. Marie even came to pick me up. Right then I thanked God for my two good friends, Charlene and Marie. We stopped for coffees on the way home as I wanted to give Mr Mc plenty of time to leave the house before I arrived there. Marie dropped me off at the door and made me promise her that I would call whenever I thought I would need her. I told her I would and I thanked her over and over as I was getting out of the car.

I walked into the house and thought to myself, Thank God Mr Mc has left and probably won't be back until the next morning. Mrs Mc was watching TV. I sat for a few minutes and chatted with her, then I saw to the children and put them all to bed. I took a shower, put my night-clothes on and finally went to bed myself. In spite of my mind still racing I was exhausted.

The next few days were a relief to me. Mrs Mc stayed home. She decided to do a lot of baking and made a big batch of spaghetti sauce. Her idea was to stock up the freezer but I was just happy to have her around.

It was just a few days later when I decided the best thing for me to do was to write to my mother and have her write a letter to the McIntyres. I would get her to tell them that she would like me to go home for a holiday because the family was missing me. I never mentioned a thing to my mother about what had been going on. I figured she would just think I was homesick. I put the letter in the mailbox right away.

One week had gone by when one morning I could see that Mrs Mc was getting ready to go somewhere. I dreaded it. The minute she left with the children I called Marie up on the phone and she promised to come right over.

I watched through the window for her car to drive up, then the minute I saw her I met her at the front door. I asked her to come into the kitchen where I had coffee waiting for her. As we walked by the bathroom, I was shocked to see the door was wide open and Mr Mc standing there stark naked. The second he saw Marie he slammed the door shut really fast. I don't believe that Marie saw him since she didn't say anything. I decided not to say anything to her until we were on the way to work. I poured her a cup of coffee, then waited until I heard him go back into his bedroom.

Marie said she would wait while I got ready for work, so once I knew he was no longer in the bathroom I went in and got ready as quickly as possible. I just wanted to get out of there.

Once we were on our way, I told Marie what I had seen. She said she hadn't noticed; maybe she wasn't looking in that direction. She advised me to try and do something as soon as I could. I told her about the letter I had sent to my mother and she said it was a shame that the only way out was to go all the way back to England. I knew I couldn't stay at Marie's as her husband was in the service and it would only be a matter of time before they would get shipped out.

The following week went by and everything went fine. Mrs Mc stayed home and managed to find enough things to do to keep busy. Finally, a week and a half went by when one afternoon Mrs Mc said she had just received a letter from my mother. Thank God, Mum wrote straight away. Mrs Mc told me that my mother wanted me to go home for a while. She looked pretty glum as she was talking to me. Finally, she said she would talk to Mr Mc when he came home for dinner.

I had to go to the café that evening, so I didn't see him until the next day at noon. The three of us sat down and they both said that it would had to have happened sooner or later, so maybe it would be a good idea for me to go for a holiday. Then I would be back for Thanksgiving and Christmas.

The next day I went to the nearest travel agent and booked my passage to England. I would have to wait a month before the next ship was to sail to Liverpool. I couldn't afford to fly, but regardless of that I preferred to sail. I was so happy to know that I would be leaving the McIntyres, I couldn't wait.

Chapter Eleven

It was approximately two weeks later when I waited on a very nice-looking guy who came into the café one evening. I couldn't help feeling attracted to him when he sat at the counter and drank his coffee. He was a quiet sort of a man and didn't say anything, only 'thank you,' as he left.

Two nights later he came in again. Once again he sat at the counter and ordered coffee but this time he was more talkative; he told me he had just arrived at the base for a six-week training programme. He was a helicopter pilot. He started to ask me about places to go and I told him he would have to go to Austin or San Antonio if he wanted to go dancing, as there was nothing to do in San Marcos.

He finally left and said he would see me later. I started to realise that I was very much attracted to him and I hoped it wouldn't be too long before he came back to the café again.

. It was approximately 8 p.m. the next night. I had finished early that day, but Marie told me he had been in the café asking for me. She told him that I worked every other night until 11 p.m.

The next evening I went to work and tried to make myself more attractive. I did my hair differently and wore a pair of my new earrings and sure enough he came in. I felt nervous, but happy to see him without making it look too obvious. I put his coffee in front of him on the counter and there was a little eye contact there as he smiled at me with that beautiful, warm smile of his.

We started to talk when he asked me if I would like to go out for dinner and dancing. I thought to myself, Wow! That would be wonderful. I told him I had to make a phone call and would let him know that evening before he left.

I waited on a couple of tables, then went and called Mrs Mc. I asked her if it would be okay if I went out the following night, which would be Saturday. She knew I hadn't had much time off to myself, so she said okay. I went to the counter and told him I could go out with him the next night. His name was Don and I knew I was going to like him very much. I couldn't wait for the next night to arrive.

The following morning I put my favourite outfit all laid aside ready for my date. It was a two-piece lavender skirt and top with black patent leather shoes and a black turtleneck under the jacket. It was my favourite thing to wear.

I started at the café at 11 a.m., and it seemed as if 7 p.m. was never going to come. Finally I finished my day shift and got a taxi home.

I took a shower, shampooed my hair and polished my nails with a soft pink nail varnish. I finally finished getting ready and had ten minutes before Don was to pick me up. Mrs Mc told me I looked really nice. I found it all to be super exciting.

It was approximately 8.30 p.m. when Don rang the front door bell. I said good night to the kids and told Mrs Mc I wouldn't be late. I opened the front door to leave. Don looked great in his beige suit and it felt so good to drive away and look forward to the evening ahead.

Don asked me where I wanted to go, but since I really hadn't been anywhere, I told him I would leave it to him. So after pondering for a few minutes he decided to go to a place in Austin that he had heard some of the guys at the base talk about. I said it sounded good to me and we headed for Austin.

We ended up at a nightclub where they had both dinner and dancing. It was so romantic to sit and have dinner with candle-light. He looked so handsome as I looked at him across the table.

Finally we strolled into the room where they were to have dancing and we found a nice cosy place to sit in the corner. We sat and talked about all kinds of things and found we were enjoying each other's company very much. We sat and talked for about half an hour, until the band started to play. I knew there wouldn't be much more talking from that point on. I just wanted to get out there and dance and that we did! We had a ball. We did everything from slow dancing to jitterbug.

I knew that I had promised to be home early, but I just didn't want the evening to come to an end. We were having too much fun. Finally after a wonderful evening they played the last waltz. We then left, but I was delighted when Don turned to me and said, 'We will have to come back here sometime.'

I smiled as I nodded okay.

Finally we reached the house. We sat and talked for a while, then I said, 'Thank you for the super time.'

As I was getting out of the car he said he would come by the café the next day and give me a ride home from work. This was the beginning of a beautiful relationship.

Don came to the café every day when I finished work. Nine times out of ten he had to take me right home because of my chores at the McIntyres', but he understood and was patient about it all. Now I started to wonder about my trip back to England and how was I going to feel about saying goodbye to him, but I decided to just wait and see what happened. There were still a few weeks to go and I thought we should make the best of them.

It was approximately a week and a half later when I received a notice in the mail informing me that Cunard Lines were going on strike, so I would have to postpone my trip until it was all over. If I hadn't met Don, I would have been disappointed but I thought that it worked out perfectly as we could spend a little more time together.

Mr Mc hadn't bothered me at all since I had started going with Don. In fact, I hardly saw him around any more. He was probably afraid I would tell Don about what he had been up to. I decided to keep it to myself. During the next few weeks Don and I had a wonderful time. Whenever I had some free time, which wasn't too often, we made the most of it.

One particular Saturday, Don picked me up early and gave me a ride to work. On the way there we passed a place where they sold new cars. I saw this beautiful red convertible in the show-room window as we drove by. I didn't say anything to Don. I just thought to myself, What a great looking car!

It was the following Saturday when Don called me to say he was on his way into town and would pick me up again to take me to work. I couldn't believe my eyes when he pulled up in the same red convertible I had seen in the shop window.

We had some good times, dancing, swimming, and going for

rides in his new car. I hated the thought of it all coming to an end.

One night when he came to the café to give me a ride home, he sat at the counter and ordered his usual cup of coffee, but I could see he had something on his mind. I asked him what was wrong, but he said he would talk about it on the way to my place.

I finished my work around the café and finally told him I was ready to leave. On the way home he told me he had received his orders to leave, as his next assignment would be in Murfreesboro, Tennessee, and that he would be leaving in a few days. I felt my heart had just dropped. He said he wanted to keep in touch with me and knew I had made arrangements to go to England. He had decided to take ten days furlough and go to Michigan to spend some time with his parents before going on to Tennessee.

We reached the McIntyres' and sat in the car talking for a while. We both hated to say goodnight, but finally he pulled me in his arms and kissed me passionately. I was afraid of Mrs Mc looking through the window and seeing us. I said goodnight to him as I composed myself before going into the house.

I couldn't sleep that night as things kept going around and around in my head. I was so mixed up, but I finally told myself that life does go on, and somehow it would all work out like it was supposed to.

It was five days later when Don called me to say he was leaving. He told me he would call me once he had arrived in Michigan, then we said our goodbyes and hung up. There seemed to be such a horrible silence that followed.

It seemed so ironic that that same afternoon I received a notice in the mail informing me that the strike was over and that my ship would be sailing from Montreal, Canada, in ten days. I couldn't believe all this was happening at the same time.

I went the next morning and bought my Greyhound bus ticket. I decided to buy a round trip and had the ticket clerk route me through Tennessee on the way back to Texas. I figured that if I ended up staying in Tennessee I could throw the rest of the ticket away. I decided to do it this way because I knew the McIntyres would want to see the ticket to make sure I would be going back to them and sure enough, they did want to look at it. Nothing more was said and I felt satisfied that everything would fall into place.

It was two days later that I received a call from Michigan. It was Don. He called to tell me he had had a good trip and that he had arrived at his parents' home and was enjoying a wonderful visit with them. I told him I had received word to sail in approximately seven days and it was at that point that he came up with a super idea. He asked me to leave as soon as possible and join him at his parents' home to spend a few days. He told me I could go through Detroit into Canada, where I would sail from Montreal. I told him I would call him back that night, as I would see what I could do. Upon hanging up the phone I immediately looked at the map and found it could be worked out perfectly. My next thought was how were the McIntyres going to feel about it. Then I decided that I didn't really care, so I went into the kitchen without any further delay and discussed it with Mrs Mc. I could sense she didn't like the idea that Don may just have ideas of taking me away from them, but she also knew that marriage had not been discussed. She also realised that I would be leaving them anyway in another week, so she reluctantly said okay.

Chapter Twelve

Within the next two days my bags were packed and I was on my way. It was wonderful to be on that bus and feel total freedom for the first time in two and a half years. I thought of my parents and the anticipation of going home. I would see my family and friends again. I thought of Don and how we could enjoy getting out and not having to be home on a certain deadline. It was a great feeling.

The bus ride went quickly. When I was an hour away from Pontiac, I called Don to let him know that I would be arriving shortly. He was over the moon. I made a quick trip to the bathroom to touch up my make-up and brush my hair. It seemed that I no sooner sat back down than the driver told us we were about to pull into the terminal.

I looked through the window and sure enough Don was there waiting for me. I put my face up to the window so he could see me, which he did right away. He waved as he smiled with that great smile of his. I departed from the bus and we started walking toward each other. We both started talking at the same time and it was wonderful to see him again. We hugged, then picked up my bags and walked to the car. Once we got inside, we held each other for at least five minutes, then we drove to his parents' home.

His parents saw us pull up into the driveway and came out to greet me. My first impression was that they appeared to be nice warm people and I took to them both instantly. We carried my bags into the small back bedroom which they had ready for me and we then had coffee in the kitchen as we talked about all kinds of things. It was the beginning of a few fabulous days.

I first went and hung up some of my clothes and took a shower and shampooed my hair. I felt great when I was all freshened up for the day. Don asked me if I would like to go for a ride and see a little of Pontiac. It was a beautiful evening as we drove around in his convertible with the top down. We drove for a couple of hours, then decided to stop at an A & W Root Beer drive-in for hamburgers. Then we took off again. Finally we decided to stop at a club and danced until 1 a.m. We were having a ball. We decided to call it a night and he drove back to his parents'. Once we were in their driveway we kissed like we never wanted to stop and I knew then that we had deep and wonderful feelings for each other.

I can't remember when I had slept as well as I did that night. Before dozing off I couldn't help but wonder if Don would come into my room, but then I shrugged it off, I knew he would have to go through his parents' room to get to mine and I decided it was better not to rush things. I always told myself that I wouldn't become sexually involved until I married.

The next few days flew by, but what a great time we had; going for drives in the country and dancing at night. We went to a couple of live shows in the evening and did a little swimming in the afternoons. There just wasn't enough time to do all the things that we would have liked to do.

Finally, it was time for me to leave. I found myself packing my suitcases once again. The next morning Don drove me to the bus station. I had to leave for Montreal, Canada, to board the ship back home. I waved to Don from the bus and blew him a kiss as the bus pulled away. We promised to write to each other as soon as he sent me his new mailing address in Tennessee. He was leaving the next day to go there.

I couldn't help but get a few tears in my eyes and yet at the same time I knew I had even more to look forward to – going home to my family.

I started to wonder how Helen and Kathleen would look now after two and a half years, also Rob. We would all have such a lot of talking to do and good times to have together.

I arrived in Montreal and got a taxi to the ship. It was so good to find my cabin and get myself sorted out. I told myself that the next few days were also going to be wonderful, just to relax and enjoy sailing across the ocean.

★

Sailing home was much better than when I sailed to the States. It was smooth and I didn't get seasick once. It was a very pleasurable trip and so relaxing, even in spite of having so many things to think about.

As we crossed the ocean I decided to just let my mind relax and look forward to going home. It was no use letting my mind race ahead. It was better to slow down and let life take its course.

Finally, after a wonderful trip we were pulling into Liverpool. I couldn't wait to get on the deck to see if I could see my family waiting for me but we were still a little too far away. It took another half an hour before we were close enough to see the people who were waiting for the ship. I started to look across the crowd and my heart began pounding with excitement when I suddenly saw my mum, Paul and my sisters and brother. They had already seen me because they were waving. Helen had something in her hand and it appeared she was trying to attract my attention with it, but I couldn't make out what it was. We started to line up to get off the ship. After about twenty minutes we were all walking down the ramp onto the dock. Oh, how exciting it was to put my feet on the ground and there was the family – they couldn't hug me enough and all talking at the same time.

We decided to go to a nearby café and have a cup of tea while the crowd dispersed. Mum had a small bottle of brandy in her handbag and she poured a little into Paul's and mine and also her own tea. It settled us down a little and it was at that point that Helen handed me the letter she had been waving. To my surprise it was a letter from Don and I thought to myself, Wow, what a day! One you never forget! We decided after a whole lot of talking that it was time to walk to the corner and get a taxi to take us home. It was super to hit Warrington and see the old familiar sights – the park and the store where I had worked, but it was especially great to arrive at our front door again.

Once we got inside, the first thing I noticed was how beautiful the house looked; so cosy with the fire going in the fireplace. Paul put on a kettle of water for us all to have another cup of tea.

I couldn't believe how Rob, Helen and Kathleen had grown. They all looked wonderful as we sat around having our tea. I opened my suitcase and handed everyone presents. They couldn't believe the nice clothes and things that I had managed to buy bit by bit from my tip money at the café.

Paul decided to put more coal on the fire. We had dinner and just sat around talking. I then put my nightclothes on after having a nice bath and a wonderful evening. We decided it was getting late, so Mum sent the kids up to bed. Just before she and Paul went upstairs I told them that I would like to sit for just a little while longer, so she poured me one more cup of tea and I put another shot of brandy in it. I then said goodnight after they both gave me a big hug.

I felt so comfortable sitting beside the fire and I decided it was time to read Don's letter. He had arrived at his new base and was settled in. He told me that he thought he was going to like it there and he was stationed with a great bunch of guys. He went on to say how much he missed me and wished I were there. He mentioned a lot of the usual things one writes in a letter; the weather was super, so on and so on. He said he would write again soon and signed off by saying, miss you and love you. I sat thinking about him for quite a while as I sipped on my tea.

The brandy was mellowing me down. I finally fell asleep in the chair. It was approximately 3 a.m. when something woke me up. It was Helen. She had crept downstairs with a pair of Paul's socks and after warming them over the coals, she put them on my feet because she was worried that I may have been cold. I smiled at her as I said thank you and she went back upstairs to bed. I dozed off again and slept until everyone came down the next morning.

We all sat and had breakfast together and I told them about Don's letter. One by one they each left the house to go to school, Paul went to work and there was just Mum and I left. We sat and talked for at least another couple of hours. I never told her about Mr Mc but she was curious as to why I wanted to leave them. I told her that two and a half years had been enough and that I wanted to see other parts of America, although at that moment I wasn't certain of just what I was going to do. She told me to have a good rest while I was back home and to just wait and see how things were going to work out. I said that would be a good idea.

as I could remember and anything else I had in the box, such as the beautiful watch that my friends at the café had given to me as a going-away present. I wasn't wearing it as the strap had broken.

Finally, the detectives left and I freshened up then walked out to the deck, I found myself a chair and just sat there thinking. I knew I would never see the jewellery again, but what was the use of worrying since I couldn't do anything about it. I really couldn't help looking up at the stars and asking, 'What's next, Lord?'

Chapter Fourteen

It was a good voyage back, smooth sailing again. Thank God I didn't get seasick. We arrived in New York before we knew it, and again I headed for the bus station. I got on the bus without delay, not wanting to hang around New York alone.

I called Don when I was just an hour away from Tennessee. He was thrilled to hear my voice on the phone. Don was there to meet me as I got off the bus at the terminal. It was wonderful to see him and the first thing we did was go and have dinner; we had such a lot to talk about.

Arrangements had been made for me to stay at the home of one of the lieutenants and his wife. The lieutenant was stationed with Don and they had become good friends. He and his wife had a spare room with a private bath that they offered to let me use. Everything was working out great.

It was only three days later that I found a job working in a restaurant so I was able to pay toward my room and board. I was off on Sundays and would help around the house.

I had only been back in the States a few weeks when Don and I got married. It wasn't anything fancy, just a short ceremony held in the Preacher's office. From there six of us went out to dinner. Don's steak was so tough that his fork slipped and his steak flew off his plate and landed in a plant pot. We laughed for a long time over that. We were able to find a cute little log cabin for rent.

We had no sooner got settled in when one day, three months later, Don called me from work to say I had better start packing as he had just received orders to go to Alaska for two years. I was sort of in shock that this had happened so soon as it seemed we had just fixed up the cabin to our liking. Then suddenly we had to move?

I made a cup of coffee and sat down while I got my head together. Pretty soon I began to get excited at the prospect of seeing such a beautiful country. It would be a whole new adventure, plus we were lucky it was a place where we could both go rather than a remote assignment where he would have to go alone. I immediately started to pack and within a week we were driving down the Alcan Highway. It took nine and a half days to reach Anchorage but the scenery was breathtaking.

We were assigned a sponsor that we called as soon as we reached the base. I thought what a super idea! He showed us to our quarters (base housing) and it was the best location on the whole base, right on the edge of the water overlooking the inlet. We were thrilled. Our sponsor then took us to his home on the base where his wife prepared us a wonderful dinner. We couldn't have been happier.

Our sponsor, Bill, and his wife, Elsie, were extremely kind. They even put us up for the night since we didn't have any furniture yet. We had to apply for base furniture the next day and it was delivered to our place during the next couple of days.

Life was very good to us there. It was a healthy life. We became avid fishermen and loved camping; my greatest feat was catching a salmon on a fly rod.

★

We had been there a little over a year when my daughter Helen was born. The year was 1957. Helen was a sickly child and she cried all day long. I had her at the doctor's all the time but most of her health problems were due to allergies that never cleared up. No matter what we gave her or did to try to make her better, she still looked so frail and never seemed to gain weight. With the best of care she pulled through it all, even though she never really learned to talk until she was five years old. She was backward in school and I even wondered if she was retarded. Specialists told me she was below average in her learning, but they gave me hope when they said she could get better as she grew older.

When our two years were up in Alaska we were given two options; one was to stay for an additional two years the other was to return to the States. We decided to stay as it was a wonderful place and we had a nice home there.

★

The following two years went by quickly. Helen seemed to be doing all right. She gained a little weight but never did get rid of her allergies. Finally, as our four years in Alaska came to a close we couldn't help wondering where we would be sent next. We were sort of hoping for a warm place like Florida or California, but to our surprise it turned out to be Duluth, Minnesota.

We felt bad saying goodbye to our neighbours, as we had become close-knit during our stay there. We all promised to keep in touch.

Once again we were lucky to get into base housing upon arriving in Duluth, We were also there a year when our son Roy was born. I dreaded to think he could be unhealthy like Helen, but he turned out to be a wonderfully healthy nine-pound baby.

We led pretty much a normal family life. We joined a church and became active members and it was there that I met someone who would become a lifelong friend. Her name was June and we were the same age. She had just had a daughter about the same time I had Roy. June and I started visiting each other a lot for coffee, or we would take the kids to the park. It was one particular afternoon when we were sitting on the park bench that we decided it was about time we asked our husbands to take us out for dinner. It suddenly occurred to both of us that our marriages had become very stale. June's husband would take off every weekend to go and stay with his eighty-year-old mother, while Don would come home from work every night, turn on the TV, then fall asleep on the living room carpet. Sometimes I couldn't wake him up so I would throw a blanket over him and find him still there the next morning.

We left the park that afternoon and it was during dinner time that we approached our husbands to take us out for an evening. We both got the same response; they would think about it.

It was five weeks later when we decided to ask them again, but still nothing doing. Two months had gone by when one day at the park, June and I decided that come Friday night we would drop the kids off at the babysitter's and go out to dinner on our own. I found myself looking forward to getting dressed up and having a nice quiet evening out. Finally when Friday evening arrived, we dropped the kids off and took off over the bridge into Superior,

Wisconsin. We found a nice restaurant and treated ourselves to a great dinner. We had such a lot to talk about. We were walking down the street back to the car when we heard music coming from a nightclub. We looked at each other with a sort of daredevil look in our eyes and we went in the back door in order not to be seen. We knew the Church wouldn't believe in something like that and neither would our husbands.

We went inside and the music was wild. I loved it. We found a little table and sat looking at the people dancing. We decided to be more daring and ordered ourselves a drink, then proceeded to look in our handbags to see if we had any mints to chew on the way home. We were safe – June had some TicTacs. We only sat there for about five minutes when a couple of guys walked over and asked us to dance. We had a blast. We stayed until almost midnight and on the way home we chewed on mints and sang, 'We're gonna dance till the midnight hour!' We both knew we would probably go back to the nightclub again.

June dropped me off at the front door and I went in quietly. The kids were asleep and Don was asleep in his usual spot on the living room floor, so I slipped off to bed.

The next morning was no different from any other morning. Don had his coffee and said, 'See you later,' then left for work.

About 10 a.m. June called me. We were excited about the fun we had had and were already planning to go again on the following Friday. The only problem was the babysitting. When we stopped to pick up our kids on the night before, we found our husbands had talked to each other on the phone and had decided to go and pick up the kids from the sitter's as it was getting late.

That afternoon June dropped by for coffee. After discussing the babysitting situation we both finally agreed that we shouldn't have to get babysitters and that our husbands should look after the kids for one lousy evening a week. After all, June's husband went away every weekend to be with his mother and my husband went to the YMCA to play handball once a week, so that was it.

That evening we both talked to our husbands about this and found it easier than we thought. We told them we would like a break too and that come Friday we would like to go browsing around the mall and then go and have dinner. They told us it was fine with them.

From that time on we lived for Friday nights. We would go in the afternoon and treat ourselves to a hairdo and we started to dress up more and bought a few new clothes.

*

During the following six months we never missed a Friday. First we would go to dinner, then hit the dance hall. Even the guys in the band would love to see us walk in and they would come and join us at our table during their break time. We never became involved with men, but we did dance up a storm! About six months later June called me one afternoon and was in tears. She told me that her husband had just called her from his office and told her that his job was thinking of transferring him to another position. They would be moving to California.

I hung up the phone and felt like I was in shock. I thought of all the fun times we had had and now she would be leaving. I felt an instant loneliness creep over me as I realised how lonely I was at home and my marriage had become so boring.

During the next four weeks we managed to get out on our Friday nights, but it left a horrible pit in the stomach to know it was coming to an end. I knew I just wouldn't enjoy going out alone; what was I going to do without my best friend?

Before we knew it we were saying our goodbyes. June and I promised each other that we would always keep in touch.

It was after she left that I went into a deep depression. I just wanted to sleep all the time. I guess you call that an escape but it's strange that a person can be married with kids and yet be horribly lonely.

Don and I started to talk about divorce, but that wasn't going to be so easy. I wasn't the kind to fight for money and the house and yet on the other hand what was I going to do with two kids? Once again I found it hard not having relatives to turn to just to help me out until I got a job and a place of my own.

After a lot of talking, Don and I decided it was best for the kids to stay with him. He had a good job and family to give him a hand, plus Helen was in an excellent school that provided her with special education for her slowness. We finally came to agreements, but I couldn't bring myself to leave the kids. I would get sick every time I made an attempt to leave. This went on for a year.

Chapter Fifteen

One day I received a wedding invitation in the mail from the McIntyres who now lived in North Carolina. Barbara, their oldest daughter, was getting married. I decided that if I went to the wedding it would be a way of making the break away from the house. Don and I agreed that this was a good idea.

I went the next day and bought a Greyhound bus ticket but it didn't just take me as far as North Carolina, from there I would travel on to California.

I called the McIntyres and told them I would be there in a few days and Mrs Mc was delighted. She said that maybe I could help her prepare for the reception.

Finally, I was on my way. I still felt terrible on the bus, but then I told myself that I was going to a wedding and I could always turn back if I realised I had made a mistake. I calmed down and at least told myself to just go and enjoy a little break, help with the wedding and take it from there.

Upon my arrival, Mrs Mc was there to meet me. She was excited to see me again after all those years and we sure had a lot to talk about.

We arrived at the house and she had a room all prepared for me. It was like turning back in time except that the kids were all grown-up. Mary followed me around the house the whole time I was there and it was as if she could still feel the bond that we had had when she was a baby. I was shocked when one afternoon there was just she and I in the house alone and she asked me if I would take her home with me. I told her that I didn't think that would be possible, but maybe some time in the future she could come and spend a holiday with me.

I felt bad for Mary. The McIntyres had written to me soon after I first left them to tell me that Mary had sort of gone into a shell and just wasn't acting right. She was three years old at the time and was never quite right afterwards. I wondered how many other kids had grown closer to their nannies or housekeepers than to their own parents. I had never once seen Mr or Mrs Mc hug or kiss her when she was a baby. I believe it had definitely affected her growth.

Barbara had grown into a beautiful young lady. She was a bag of nerves during that particular time, but I guess that's normal when you are planning for your wedding. The child that they had after I had left them was now fourteen years old. Her name was Jane. David, the son, arrived the day after I got there. I couldn't believe how tall he was. The little kid I had taken care of years before now towered over me and he had to be at least six foot four inches.

Finally, it was Saturday and the wedding was to be that afternoon. I could have died when Mrs Mc asked Mr Mc to give me a ride to the reception hall as she wanted me to put some decorations on the tables and just sort of check on things.

Once he and I were in the car, he started to talk nastily. He talked about what he had seen in the shower years before and on and on he went. The one thing I felt nervous about was that he might decide to drive to some secluded area and try something – but thank God he didn't! I couldn't wait to get out of that car. As we pulled up to the reception hall I knew I would be sorry in a way for going there. Somehow we give people the benefit of the doubt that maybe they have changed. What a joke! In spite of all this I also knew that by going to the wedding it was my break from home. My marriage wasn't happy any more.

I stayed at the hall about two hours and did all that I could possibly do to finish things up. Then I called Mrs Mc to come and pick me up so that I could get ready for the wedding.

The next couple of hours were all spent getting dressed. Everyone looked beautiful. We left the house at 3.45 p.m.

The wedding went super, but as I observed it all I went through so many mixed emotions. I would look at Mrs Mc and the kids and think what a great looking family, but then I would look at Mr Mc and think of his deceitfulness and wonder just what his family would think if they knew what a monster they had living with them. It was as if he didn't belong at that wedding and especially walking that beautiful bride down the aisle! I was happy when the whole thing was over. I went to bed that night and figured I would stick around for one more day and help clean up the hall. I also decided to travel on to California rather than go back home. It was too soon and I wanted more time to think about things. Finally, I fell into a deep sleep and I was too tired to think any more.

The next day we all pitched in and got everything back to normal. I re-packed my suitcase and wondered what that long journey on the bus was going to be like. I figured it would take at least three days to reach California.

I called Don that afternoon and everything was fine back there. I told him what I had decided to do and he agreed that maybe a break would give us a chance to really think everything over. I told him I was leaving for California the next morning and that I would call him from along the way. The conversation was good and I knew that if all else failed, we would always communicate by phone or letter and remain friends.

I was so happy to see Monday morning arrive. I got up, took a shower, had coffee, and wondered who was going to give me a ride to the bus station. Thank God it wasn't Mr Mc – he left early for his office and Mrs Mc asked David to drop me off at the station.

Chapter Sixteen

It was a long ride to California, but I kept myself occupied reading magazines and rapping to different people on the bus. Finally, after a long journey I arrived in San Francisco. I was never so happy to see anyone in my life as I was to see June! She was there waiting for me and we were so excited we couldn't stand it. We decided on the way to her house to get off at a certain exit and go and have a drink and we sat for two hours talking about everything we could think of. I could see that June also was very unhappy in her marriage and her husband was miserable since he could no longer visit his mother at weekends.

It was about midnight when we arrived at June's house. Her husband, Chad, was still up and helped me with my suitcases. We didn't stay up long since I was tired from the journey and Chad had to get up for work the next morning.

The next day I felt very refreshed after a good night's sleep. After four cups of coffee I decided to look and see what the job situation looked like in the newspaper. I didn't find much that first day, but to my surprise the next day I came across an ad where someone was looking for a person to live in, to do housework and take care of three kids. I thought, Oh boy! Here we go again, but since I didn't have a car or much money, maybe this would be a good thing.

I called up right away and to my surprise I was hired. The woman of the house, Mrs Brendel, asked if I could start the following Monday. I told her that would be perfect as it gave me a chance to have a few days' rest.

By the time Monday rolled around I was happy to leave June's house. She and I got along fine, but I could feel the tension between her and Chad. You can't help wondering what happens to these marriages, but then again, what about the times we would ask our husbands to go places with us and just enjoy life? It was all to no avail.

I moved into the Brendels' on the Monday as arranged. The job was identical to the McIntyres except that I didn't have to put up with any harassment from Mr Brendel.

There was only one occasion that Mr Brendel got a little out of hand. It was on a Saturday night and I was babysitting their kids, I put them to bed around 9 p.m., then sat in the den watching TV. Mr and Mrs Brendel came home around midnight and it appeared to me that they had been out for a few drinks and got into an argument. Mrs Brendel muttered goodnight to me and went straight upstairs to bed. He came into the den and sat down in the big easy chair and he asked me if I would fix him a cup of coffee, which I did. As I handed the coffee to him he reached for it with one hand and with the other, he took my arm and started to pull me toward him. I just calmly told him to cool it, that he had had a drink and would only feel embarrassed the next day. At that point I said goodnight and walked upstairs. I thought to myself, I'm not going through that bloody rubbish again!

I didn't get to see June very much, but I had been at my job about six months when she called me to say that Chad had just packed up his job, gone home, took a suitcase of clothes and left. I couldn't believe it, but then again I guess I could. They had had problems for a long time.

I never saw Chad again. The last we heard of him was that he had gone to the airport and taken the next plane to Minnesota to go and stay with his mother for a while before getting another job and relocating.

I had one and a half days off a week and June asked me to spend my night off at her place to keep her company. We would buy a bottle of wine, play some records and sit around the fireplace and talk for hours. She talked about getting a job and she would have to go to work in order to keep the house.

It was about two weeks after Chad left that June got a good waitress job that also made good tips. We were both making it as best we could. She started to have an occasional evening out and was enjoying life.

It seemed like no time at all had gone by when June met a super guy named Jack. He adored June and he did all the things for her that Chad had never done. He was always buying her presents and taking her places.

I stayed at the Brendels' for eight months. During that time I saved enough money to buy a second-hand car and I had another job all lined up before leaving them, plus a trailer to rent. June and Jack helped me move into my trailer. It was great to finally have a place of my own. Once I got settled I started on my new job that was also at a restaurant. I shall call the restaurant Phill's Place. I had two of the best bosses in the world. They were in partnership and had been for years. Phill's Place was very popular for its great food.

I remember one day when Phillip took me aside and said, 'You live alone, Pat, don't go buying groceries. Help yourself to whatever you want.'

Naturally I couldn't do that, so he started putting a container with my dinner in it next to my handbag every day just before I left. Sometimes there would be a loaf of bread and a salad. They were so good to me. Phillip was a sweetheart and had such a great sense of humour. We were always having a good laugh about something. His partner, Mark, was the more serious one, but just as great to get along with. I developed a big crush on Mark. He was just the kind of guy I would have liked to have had for myself; responsible, hard working and a real fox to look at. Mark never knew my feelings for him. He and Phillip were both married with kids. I would go and do my job and just keep to myself. I always had that reserved way about me in spite of the good laughs we would have from time to time.

I had worked at Phill's Place about three months when one Friday afternoon I had just arrived home from work when the phone rang. It was June and she asked me if I would like to go to a dance with her and Jack.

She said there was supposed to be a good band at this certain club. I said, 'Sure, it sounds great.'

I met June and Jack about 9 p.m. and it was great to get out and be with company and sure enough the band was super.

As the evening went on I couldn't help noticing this guy at the next table. He had the greatest looking eyes I had ever seen and was sitting with five other people.

I didn't want him to catch me looking, but as I leaned over and whispered to June and Jack to take a look at his eyes, he saw us. He looked a little embarrassed and probably wondered what we were looking at.

The band finally took a break, but during the next set the guy with the eyes came and asked me for a dance. The next thing he did was wander over to our table and asks us if he could join us. He said he would like to buy us a round of drinks. We said, sure, we didn't mind if he would like to sit with us. We couldn't really talk much because the band was kind of loud, so we just sat and had a couple of drinks and danced.

Finally, it was 1 a.m., and everyone started to leave. Eyes, whose name was Bob, walked to the car with me and he asked me if I would like to go to dinner with him in a couple of days, which would be Sunday. I figured I might as well as I hadn't dated once since breaking up with Don. I gave him my phone number, then said goodnight.

*

It was around 4 p.m. on Sunday when Bob called. I gave him instructions on how to get to my place so that he could pick me up. That was my first big mistake.

I took a shower and got ready to go. He picked me up around 5.30 p.m. We went to the same club that we had met in two nights before and we sat and ordered a drink. He appeared to be very nervous but the drink started to loosen him up. He started to tell me that those people he was sitting with on the Friday were all family members. One was his sister, another was his brother, and so on. They had decided to get together and take Bob out on the town since he had just been released from prison a few days previously.

He told me he had been locked up for eleven years. I was shocked, but didn't show it. I never asked him what he had done wrong. I figured that was up to him to tell me if he wanted to. I knew at that moment that I didn't want any kind of relationship with this man. He had a lot of catching up on life to do. I told him that he had paid a heavy price for whatever he had done, but to go straight now and enjoy his freedom, I figured I would be a friend and try to encourage and guide him as best I knew how.

Finally, the conversation came to an end and we decided to go and have dinner. From there he said he had to drop by his sister's where he was staying at the time and then he would drop me off at my trailer.

I waited in the car while he ran in to see his sister. A few minutes later she came to the door and motioned for me to go in. She introduced herself as Brenda and her husband's name was Edward. It appeared to me that they were very good to Bob. Brenda had a job all lined up for him, she had bought new clothes which were hanging in the closet, and even bought a second-hand car so he would have his own wheels. We stayed for about ten minutes and then I had to get home. Just before we left, Brenda handed me her phone number and asked me to stop by the next day for coffee after I got off work. I thanked her and left.

I called her the next day and told her I was so tired, especially since I had to get up at 4.30 a.m. I had been given the keys to the restaurant and it was my responsibility to go in early and start preparing for the breakfast shift.

I told Brenda that I would stop by the next day. We had a ten-minute conversation on the phone and she sounded very concerned about Bob and said how worried she was. She just wanted him to do right in life and go straight.

As time went on, I found that Bob was becoming a real pain. He would call on the phone or stop by my trailer at all hours of the night. I told him that he had to go out and date girls and have a good time and not to cling to me as I only wanted to be friends.

Brenda and I became pretty close. I would often go over to her place and have coffee with her and Ed. We started to worry more about Bob as he was always getting stopped for speeding and spent a night in jail for drinking and driving. She also noticed he was stealing from the warehouse where he worked. I had the feeling that Bob was stalking me. Once in a while I would visit June and when I got home there would be pages of a newspaper taped all over my door and also a cinder block in my parking space. They were things to let me know he had been there. I thought it to be very odd behaviour.

It was one particular Friday night that Brenda called me up and asked me to go for a drink with her. She sounded fed up. Ed had suggested that she should call me and go out for a while and he would stay home with their two kids.

Brenda left Ed with the phone number of the club where we were going to be, then she came to pick me up. We had been at the club for about an hour and a half when Ed called and asked to speak with Brenda. When she came back to the table, she said Ed sounded scared to death. He told her that Bob had been out but went back to the house drunk. He was mad because we were out and he threatened that he would take my car and crash it if I didn't get home within the hour. I told Brenda not to worry, that Bob had been drinking and he couldn't possibly take my car because he didn't have the car keys. We stayed for one more hour, then decided to leave. I had Brenda drop me off on the street side rather than go around the back to my trailer. I said goodnight and not to worry so much. I told her I would call her the next day.

I cut through the middle of the trailer park and when I got to mine I almost fainted on the spot. My car was there in its usual spot, but completely demolished. I couldn't even imagine how Bob got the car back to my place from the spot he had done this. I noticed the lights on my trailer were out and I knew I had left them on when I left. I walked in and found Bob sitting there on the lounge chair drinking a bottle of beer. I guessed that he had broken into my trailer and found my extra set of car keys. Strangely enough he had managed to get into my trailer without breaking the lock on the door.

He said, 'Where the hell have you been?'

I took one look at him and could have killed him on the spot. I grabbed his hair and tried to throw him out but he smashed the beer bottle on the counter and I thought, Right then, that's curtains. I thought for sure he was going to come at me with the broken bottle, but he smashed the rest of it on the sink.

We got into a hell of a fight. During the scuffle we both fell against the glass sliding door, breaking it into a thousand pieces. Thank God the drapes were closed. I'm sure they protected us from being seriously injured. Breaking the door made me even more furious. I seemed to have mustered up an incredible

amount of strength that came with anger I opened my trailer door
and slung him through it so hard I thought I had probably killed
him for sure. He started to get up and come towards the door. I
slammed it in his face and put the chain on; then I thought in
horror that he might try climbing through the broken window. I
grabbed the phone and screamed to him that I was calling the
cops. That must have scared him because he was on parole and he
knew right then that he was in serious trouble. I held on to the
phone and everything went silent. I looked through the window
and saw him staggering toward the street. I don't know where his
car was; he must have been sly enough to hide it on the next street
over.

I immediately called Brenda and told her what had happened.
She went hysterical. I told her I should have called the cops and it
was only because of her that I didn't. She then heard a car pull up
outside and quickly said she would call me back, then hung up. I
poured myself a good stiff drink, then sat and looked around. I
put my head in my hands and thought, This is nothing short of a
horrible nightmare. I looked at all the destruction that had
happened in just one evening. I couldn't even begin to understand
where all the blood had come from and I couldn't figure out why
this had to happen to me. I hadn't bothered a soul and only meant
to be a friend to Bob.

Things had been going so good for me with my job, my life,
everything. I started to clean up the mess, which took me at least
an hour. I took the mattress off my bed and put it where the
sliding glass door had been. I finally decided to take a nice hot
shower and I no sooner had got back into the living room than
the phone rang. It was Brenda. She had just got home from taking
Bob to the emergency room where he had to have ten stitches on
his hand. It must have happened when he smashed the bottle. She
finally talked him into going to bed and I told her once again that
I would call her the next day, then said goodnight.

I sat in the armchair all night and I couldn't sleep a wink. I
couldn't wait for daylight.

It was about 7 a.m. when I heard someone outside. I looked
through the window and saw it was Brenda standing there
looking at my car.

I opened the door and she came in. We sat and had a long talk and I told her to have a talk with Bob. I said I didn't want him coming to my trailer any more and I didn't even want him calling me on the phone.

Brenda felt terrible about the whole thing. She said that maybe I should have gone ahead and called the police.

I said, 'Yeah, I know I should have.'

We had all tried to help Bob go straight and didn't want to see him go back to prison.

She said, 'God knows where he is going to end up but I can't take much more of it.' Before she left she told me not to worry; she said she would come by early Monday morning and give me a ride to work and also take me back home in the afternoon.

When she arrived back home she called me to say that Ed was going to try to find me another second-hand car. I was thankful to have them both behind me and giving me all the help they could. I decided the next thing I had to do was call the junkyard and have them come and haul the car away. I didn't want anything around to draw attention; all I needed was to get kicked out of my trailer. My car was hauled away within the hour. I waited another half-hour and then went to the landlady's trailer that was at the end of the park. I couldn't bring myself to tell her all that had happened so I had to tell her a white lie. I said I had tripped on the rug and fallen against the glass sliding door. I apologised and said I would pay for it. The landlady was very nice about the whole thing and said she hoped I hadn't got hurt. She also said she would get it seen to right away. I thanked her and left.

Brenda had a long talk with Bob and told him to stay away from my trailer and that he had caused me a lot of grief, not to mention all the expense. Bob didn't come back but did keep calling me on the phone, but I would just hang up on him.

During that following week Ed managed to find me another car, thank God. Also, the landlady had my glass sliding door fixed. It felt good that things were getting back to normal.

★

It was one week later, on a Monday night when my phone kept

ringing. Bob had gone to a bar after he left work and he was trying to get me to go and meet him for a drink. I still kept hanging up. I thought to myself that there was one more thing I had to do; have my number changed.

I finally went to bed that night and fell into a deep sleep. It was around 11 p.m. when I was awakened by the phone ringing. I almost didn't answer it, but thought that someone else might be trying to reach me. I picked up the phone and it was Brenda. She was so upset that she could hardly speak. She had just finished talking to the police and evidently Bob got into an argument with a couple of guys at the bar and the bartender asked the three of them to leave. Once outside, they continued to argue. Bob had a gun tucked in his belt underneath his sweater, God knows where he got it, none of us knew he had it. During the argument the gun went off, but luckily no one was injured. Needless to say, the police were called and Bob was arrested. Due to his record, Bob was kept in jail, then eventually transferred to another prison to serve more time.

There was still one more shock to come. About two months later I was once again awakened by the phone ringing. This time it was Ed. He said they had just been notified that Bob had succumbed to a very brutal attack by one of the other inmates and he had been stabbed fifteen times. I immediately got dressed and went over to Brenda's. She was so pale and sick and I felt sorry for her especially since her other brother had been killed in a car wreck the year before. I tried to console her but at one point she said maybe Bob was better off dead since he couldn't take control of his life and would have always been in some kind of trouble.

I stayed with her for about two hours, then had to go home and try to rest before going to work early the next morning. I couldn't sleep a wink and in one way I felt relieved that it was all over, yet I also felt bad to think of a life so wasted. There was one consolation and that was knowing that everyone had tried. There was nothing else that anyone could have done for him.

The family had a small private funeral for Bob that I attended. On my way home afterward, I thought how it had all been a horrible chapter in my life. Now I just wanted to go on in peace. It was over.

Chapter Seventeen

The weeks and months went by. I more or less buried myself in work. Every weekend I would buy something nice for my trailer and it looked really beautiful. I especially liked the two small lamps I had bought for the living room. I couldn't stand bright lights so I put pink light bulbs in the lamps, which made the place so warm and cosy looking at night.

Different things started to take place – my divorce became final and so did June's. She and Jack were making plans to be married in the Spring. I continued to visit Brenda and once in a while we would all have dinner together. I never told June about the bad episode I had had with Bob. She would only have been worried and upset and it was water over the dam. I always enjoyed my visits with June. We had so many good laughs around the fireplace and I felt that life in general was on the upswing again.

I sat in my armchair one night listening to my stereo. I found I was asking myself a question and that was how could I spend some of my free time. I never liked life to become too routine week in and week out, when I suddenly hit on an idea. Why not take up tap-dancing again? That was something I had enjoyed as a kid. It was a great pastime and it would also keep me in shape.

I called up a few dance studios when I got home from work the following day and found one close by. I bought myself a nice new pair of silver tap shoes and started tap lessons the following Saturday morning. From there I went to an exercise class. I never felt so good in my life. Tap-dancing was something that came easily to me and I went from beginners' to the advanced class within the first month.

We started putting on shows at small theatres around the area. It was great. I never hit the big time, but it was all enough to make me feel good about myself.

One year later on 4th July weekend, 1973, my boss decided to close the restaurant because a lot of the staff were going away, plus he himself wanted to get away for a few days. I decided to make good use of the time off, so Saturday, after I arrived home from my tap-dancing class, I thought I would give my trailer an extra good cleaning and at the same time I was wondering what to wear to the club that night. It was a beautiful day, eighty degrees and sunny and I figured my pink off-the-shoulder dress would be perfect.

It was about 2 p.m., and I had almost finished cleaning when a knock came on the door. I peeped through the window and saw it was Mark, my boss. I opened the door and he said he came by to pick up the keys to the restaurant, as he needed to get in to collect a bucket of ice for his other restaurant. He had a reception going on and he was running short. I asked him to step inside while I went to get them out of my handbag. He sat down at the kitchen table, which was just to the right of the door, then I handed over the keys and offered him a cold drink. He sat talking for about ten minutes. He looked around and told me how great my trailer looked.

Finally he got up to leave and he said he would bring the keys back some time over the weekend. I walked to the door with him and his arm accidentally brushed against mine. I pretended not to notice as I said, 'Bye, see you later.' I couldn't help feeling guilty for the way that I felt. As I closed the door a surge of excitement came over me and I thought, God I wish that guy was mine. What a hunk!

During the next hour I was battling with my feelings. Finally I told myself to forget it, that he was a married man and I sure as hell didn't want to go breaking someone's marriage up. Then I pushed it all out of my mind. I put the finishing touches on my trailer, pressed my pink dress and decided to take a nap.

I fell into a deep sleep until about 6.30 p.m. I got up and fixed a sandwich and sat around for a while. Then I decided it was time to start getting ready to go out. I had managed to get a super suntan and I put my pink dress on feeling like a million dollars. As I was driving down the street toward the club, I thought to myself, Wow, what a wonderful balmy night!

I arrived at the club in time to find my usual little table next to the wall was vacant. I sat and ordered myself a drink and said hi to the usual people that I saw every weekend. It was a great band and I just sort of danced the night away. I stayed until midnight, then decided to go home. The club stayed open until 1 a.m. but I enjoyed going home to listen to my stereo for an hour before calling it a night.

I had been home about ten minutes when the phone rang. I couldn't imagine who would be calling me at that hour. It was Mark and he said he had called several times but I wasn't home. He asked me if it was all right if he stopped by with the keys, as he had just closed his restaurant and might not have a chance the next day, as he was expecting another busy time. I said, sure, that would be all right.

About ten minutes later I heard his car pull up. I opened the door and he came in. He had a brown paper bag in his hand and as he stepped into the kitchen he pulled out a bottle of brandy and asked me if I would like a drink. I said sure and fixed us both one. We sat at the kitchen table and talked. He was telling me about his busy day at the restaurant and I was talking about the fun evening I had just had.

Finally we finished our drink, and then he said, 'How about one for the road?'

I asked him if his wife would be wondering where he was but he told me that she went away every weekend to their summer cabin. I thought at that point, What a strange relationship, but didn't say anything. I got up and fixed us another brandy. As I turned to put the drinks down on the table he was standing behind me about a foot away. His fabulous body looked like a vision against the soft pink lights and I started trembling as he moved toward me.

He laid his hand on my naked shoulder and I felt his warm breath on my neck as I drew him toward me. His arms felt so wonderful – all my barriers were down. I couldn't think of the right and the wrong but I was vulnerable and I wanted him. We made love all night long and all I could think of was how I would like to lock my trailer door and throw the key away. What a chemistry we had; something super special! Finally he left at 8 a.m. He said he would call me and after he left the guilt set in. I started thinking about his wife and kids and yet at the same time I couldn't wait to see him again.

Every time the phone rang I couldn't wait to answer it. Mark called me every night. He started coming by every Wednesday, but didn't stay. Weekends were becoming hot and heavy. How I wished he belonged to me and yet there was a certain excitement about the whole thing.

Chapter Eighteen

During hunting season he went to Reno for a week. He left on a Saturday and called me the next day. He had already caught a deer so had nothing to do for the rest of the week. He asked me to call Jean, a girl that used to work my job, to see if she could fill in for me. He wanted me to catch a bus and go and join him. I was so excited at the prospect of being alone with him for a whole week that I couldn't think straight. I called Jean and she said she would be happy to fill in for me. Then I called my boss, Phill, and told him I had to take a few days off. He said that as long as I had someone to take my place it would be fine. I packed a small suitcase and called a cab to the bus station. Mark had called me back so I told him what time to meet me.

The bus arrived in Reno at midnight and Mark was there to meet me. It was the beginning of a fabulous week. It was late, so we went straight to the room he had booked where he had snacks and a bottle of champagne waiting. We took a shower and put our satin robes on. It was fun sitting on the bed laughing, talking and drinking the champagne. The lovemaking was magical. It was as if we couldn't get enough of each other. Every day was great. We hit the casinos and went to the live shows in the evening. We didn't want the week to end, but finally it did and we drove home together.

The routine went back to being the same with the phone calls every night, his stopping by on Wednesday and the passionate weekends. We had a year-long romance. I adored Mark and I know his feelings were deep for me, but I began to realise that the relationship wasn't going anywhere. I couldn't stand the fact that when he left my place he was going back to his wife. I started to do some heavy thinking and I realised that my life wasn't getting anywhere. I needed a change and thought I'd better do it before he got caught. I also decided not to tell Mark, as I just wanted to make a break and start anew.

The big decision was where I went from there. My brother Rob, who was a grown young man by then, had recently moved to the States. He was living in Rhode Island on the East Coast. I called him and told him I felt like a change and wanted to leave California. Rob was thrilled at the prospect of our seeing each other again. He told me he had a nice two-bedroom apartment and I could stay at his place as long as I wanted.

I immediately gave two weeks notice on my job. I knew Mark would find out, so I packed everything and went to stay with June and Jack until it was time to leave.

★

The next two weeks went by quickly. June gave me a ride to the airport and along the way I told her how happy I was for her and Jack, and how super their marriage was. She wished me all the very best as she hugged me at the airport. Our tears were pretty heavy as we said goodbye. I began to think that my whole life was made up of both of them.

There I was on a plane again, sitting back thinking I missed Mark something awful, but what was the use; I knew I had done the right thing. I also thought of Phill, my boss, and how hurt he looked when I gave in my notice. He told me before I left that if things didn't work out on the East Coast that he would have me back if I returned to California.

I already missed June and Jack. We had a lot of laughs together and they were good friends, but I felt a lot of peace knowing they had found each other and were extremely happy. Finally I made a big decision. I told myself that I would never get involved with a married man again. It wasn't right and went nowhere.

I arrived at the Boston airport, and there was Rob to meet me. I couldn't believe how he had grown into such a handsome young man. We couldn't wait to get out of the airport, we had so much catching up to do. I told him I could go for a brandy.

He said, 'Me too,' so we stopped and had a couple. We eventually left the bar and arrived at his apartment. It was beautiful and I couldn't believe how immaculate he kept it. It must have been that strict upbringing from Beatrice.

There was so much to talk about that we didn't even sleep that night. There wasn't too much he could tell me about our family back in England. Mum wrote to me all the time and gave me all the news. In fact, people used to marvel how she could get a thirteen-page letter into a regular size envelope. Rob told me how beautiful our sisters were. He said they looked like movie stars. Kathy married her high school sweetheart and she had joined the theatre as a wonderful actress.

I was shocked when Rob started to tell me things about Helen. I realised at that point that Mum had held a lot back from me because she knew I would worry. Helen had been married twice and both marriages ended in divorce. After the second one broke up, Helen threw in the sponge and sort of gave up on life. She was drinking heavily and had even spent time in jail for drink-driving. On one occasion she had taken a bunch of pills and washed them down with gin then got in her car and crashed through a big store window. She had been cut up pretty badly but survived the terrible accident. I couldn't help thinking of my grandma and how she had gone to the dogs after losing those three children. Maybe Helen was following in her footsteps.

I finally looked at the clock, and it was 6.30 a.m.! Rob and I decided it was time to get some rest. I should have gone out like a light, but instead I felt very disturbed. I wondered what Helen's problems could be doing to my mum and Paul's health. Mum had had two nervous breakdowns and she didn't need another one. Since I couldn't sleep I got up and decided to write a long letter to my mum. I told her I had moved to the East Coast and that I would be staying with Rob for a short while. I told her that Rob had told me about Helen and asked her if there was anything I could do. I would have called her right then, but they didn't have a phone. They couldn't afford one.

I mailed the letter that morning, and four days later I received a phone call from my mum who was calling from a pay phone. She was delighted to hear that Rob and I were together, but was a little annoyed that Rob had worried me with Helen's problems. She said there was nothing that I could do and said the whole family had tried to talk sense into her or tried to help in some way. I thanked her for calling and said I would write again soon.

I spent a few days with Rob before looking for a job. I needed a break, but once again things started to fall into place for me. I found a little second-hand car five days after I got there, a job in a diner which was only part-time and a couple of housekeeping jobs to make a little extra money. Within one month I also found a cute little apartment, so I was all set.

My life became pretty stabilised. Things were going well for me and I became more of a loner than I had ever been. Rob and I would visit each other from time to time or go for a drink on a Friday night.

Chapter Nineteen

The years seemed to slip by. I did fly home and spent a wonderful Christmas with Mum and Paul. Helen was impossible. I tried so hard to get through to her, but to no avail. It was something we all had to live with, but it wasn't easy. She affected the whole family and each of us found ourselves worrying what she was doing to our nerves.

That was my last trip over there until the year 1981. It was 16th November when I arrived home from work and received one of those phone calls that everyone dreads. My sister Kathleen called me to say that my stepfather Paul had had a massive coronary and died very suddenly. I was heartsick as I had always loved Paul dearly. I called the diner and told my boss that I had to take some time off as there had been a death in the family. He said sure, they would manage somehow.

I got a flight home the next day. My sister Kathy met me in Manchester and I asked her to tell me exactly what had happened. It didn't happen at home. Paul was buying the morning news-paper at the corner store when he was suddenly struck and he was dead before they got him out of there.

We finally reached my mum's house and she was so happy and relieved to see me. I felt so sorry for her; she looked so alone in that big house. I hugged her for a long time and told her not to worry, that everything would be all right. Kath fixed us a cup of tea and we sat and talked for quite a while.

I couldn't believe the speed with which everything took place during the three weeks I was there. First came the funeral, then I asked Mum if she had thought of putting the house up for sale. I couldn't see her living there alone as it was on a very quiet dark street and she would have been a nervous wreck. Mum put the house up for sale right away and Kath found a flat, which she and I painted. We managed to find someone with a truck to remove Mum's belongings and things fell into place in an unbelievable way. By the time I was ready to fly back to the States, Mum was all set and comfortable. I felt good knowing everything possible had been done and she would be all right. I returned to the States and couldn't thank my boss enough for giving me the time off.

Chapter Twenty

Once again life went on. Over the years I had never got involved with anyone as far as a relationship. I had never really got over Mark. Strangely enough, in spite of the circumstances, he had been the love of my life and I never stopped thinking about him.

Two years after Paul died, I worried to death about Mum. Kath started to write me letters, telling me that Helen was spending a lot of time at my mum's house. I knew that couldn't be good for Mum. I figured she was drinking heavily whenever Helen was there and it was due to her being lonely. The thing that I didn't like was that Helen was stealing money out of my mum's purse.

It was one particular Saturday night that Kathleen called me, so upset she could hardly talk. She told me that Helen had gone to Mum's house that evening and she was drunk and started arguing with Mum. She grabbed my mother's glasses off her face and broke them then smashed her TV. Kath said she had to take Mum to the hospital with a bad nosebleed and she would be in there a couple of days.

I couldn't stand it any more. I told Kath to tell Mum when she picked her up from the hospital, that I was flying back to get her and that I would be bringing her back to the States. I figured I couldn't put my boss through any more of taking time off, so I quit my job and once again found myself flying back home.

Within two weeks we had all of Mum's furniture and everything sold. I never once saw Helen to tell her what I thought of her but she was back in jail again, serving six months for drinking and driving.

I brought Mum back to the States. Thank God I had a nice apartment. It was small but we found it to be big enough for the two of us and we were very comfortable there.

★

It was October 1983 when I brought her to the States, Christmas was around the corner and I wanted it to be the best one that she had ever had. I was obsessed with making her happy and I wanted to make up for all the years we had been apart.

Christmas was wonderful. There were so many presents that there was hardly room to walk in the apartment. Rob had bought a lot of them himself, and between the two of us we figured it would take three days for her to open them all. It was a Christmas to remember. I tried to think of all the things to do to make her happy and enjoy life. I knew she was hurting inside. She felt as if she had abandoned Helen who was so sick and I thought it best not to mention her name. Once Christmas was over, I thought she would love to go to the *Icecapades*. She had never been to one in her life so I went and bought two tickets, but didn't tell her about them. Finally when it was time to go I just told her to get ready as we were going out for a while.

We arrived at the Civic Centre and found our seats. She still couldn't imagine what it was all about but finally the beautiful coloured lights went on and the show started. She was mesmerised and it was a joy to see her face. She loved every minute of it and never stopped talking about it for a whole week.

It was early April and we were driving down the street when she suddenly spotted a bunch of tables on a person's lawn and asked me what it was. It was a yard sale, something else she had never seen so I pulled over and told her to look around. She couldn't believe that things were so cheap. I got a kick out of watching her buy things, and she talked all the way home about how she had paid £8 at Marks and Spencers in England for a red blouse and had just found one equally as nice for fifty cents. She was a trip!

It was 21st April, a Saturday night. Mum always stayed home on Saturdays because she enjoyed the TV programmes, but for some reason she felt like getting out for a while. I suggested going to the movies, but she said she felt like going to a place where there was music. I told her there was a good country and western band down the road at Twinks Tavern. I told her it was a good place to go as they never had any fights or any other kind of problems there.

She said, 'It sounds good. Let's go.'

We got dressed up and went there. The band was great. There was one thing I noticed that night; Mum refused a couple of guys who asked her to dance. It wasn't like her – she loved to dance, but I shrugged it off, thinking that maybe she was a little tired and just wanted to relax.

Finally we decided to leave about 12.30 a.m. We got in the car and Mum said how she enjoyed getting out for a while and remarked on how good the band was. We got halfway down the street when all of a sudden she started to babble. She was talking in riddles, then she slumped over. Her head was resting against the door on her side. It all happened so fast I was in shock for the first ten seconds, then panic set in. I found myself saying, 'Oh, God, help me. What's wrong?' I thought she must have had a stroke, I didn't know the way to the hospital and I almost passed out from nerves. I decided to turn around and run back to the tavern. I asked the bartender to call the Rescue Squad. He sent a couple of off-duty policemen out to see if there was anything they could do. They felt her pulse and shook her gently to see if they could bring her around. She opened her eyes for a brief moment, but was out of it; she couldn't talk or anything. The Rescue Squad arrived within minutes and one of the policemen was good enough to ask me if I would like him to drive me to the hospital, I couldn't thank him enough.

We waited for two and a half hours for the doctor to come and tell us what was happening. Finally he came and told me that things didn't look too good, that Mum wasn't responding in any way. I couldn't believe this was happening. She was fine one minute, and now this?

We continued to wait to see if there would be any changes, but it was 7 a.m. when once again the doctor came. He looked a little happier as he said she was showing signs of improvement. He said we should go home and get some rest and check back in the afternoon. I thanked the policeman again as he dropped me off at my car.

I arrived home and I felt drained. I sat drinking coffee and smoked cigarettes like you wouldn't believe. I knew it was no use to lie down so I just paced the floor for hours. Finally I looked at the clock and decided it was time to take a shower and get ready to go back to the hospital. While I was doing that I thought about Rob. Of all of the times for him to be away for the weekend it had to be then, but thank God he was due home that night.

I arrived back at the hospital and I couldn't believe my eyes when I walked into Mum's room. She was sitting up in bed and a big smile broke out on her face when she saw me. I gave her a big hug and told her everything would be all right. Her speech was still all mixed up and I wondered if it was going to stay like that. I didn't notice any paralysis that usually comes with a stroke so I thought that maybe she had just had a mild one.

I sat and talked to her for about half an hour and then went looking for the doctor. He was on another floor when I had first arrived, but finally I got a chance to talk to him. He assured me that her speech would return, but he couldn't tell me much more until they had run a whole bunch of tests.

About a week later the doctor took me aside and gave me the grim news. He told me that Mum didn't have long to live as she had a massive brain tumour. Right then my heart broke in two. He said the only thing they could do for her was to give her radiation treatment but it wasn't a cure. It would only prolong her life a little.

I couldn't bring myself to tell Mum what was wrong. I told her she was suffering from nervous exhaustion from the trip and trying to make a new start. I kept assuring her that everything would be all right and she just needed a good rest. At least that seemed to pacify her and it was better than telling her she was dying.

It was a few days later when the doctor called me to say Mum had refused further radiation, which meant she could no longer stay in the hospital. When I arrived at the hospital that afternoon, the doctors had a long talk with me. They told me I wouldn't be able to care for her at home and said the only answer would be to put her in a nursing home.

I cried all the way home and called my kids to tell them the rotten news. My daughter immediately took two weeks off from her job and flew out to be with me. She was such a comfort to me. I took her to see Mum right away. I knew as she entered

Mum's room that it would be another tearjerker. Mum hadn't seen her in twenty years. Even the nurses were wiping their eyes.

The following two weeks went by too fast. My daughter had to leave, and Mum had been transferred to the home. Every morning while doing my housekeeping jobs, I thought how lonely and afraid Mum must be. She not only had moved to a strange country, but also in the matter of a few months had ended up being shoved into a nursing home.

I became angry as I told myself that I had brought her over and no way was she going to be stuck in that place. I knew I had to get her out of there as much as I could, so every afternoon right after lunch time I would go and put her in the wheelchair and push her for miles down the back streets. It was always a bonus when the ice cream truck came by.

*

Finally it was Saturday morning, 16th September. I received a call saying Mum had taken a turn for the worse and I had better get down there. I was there in a flash. Mum didn't know me. I looked at her and thought how she had been. I never saw her cry once. I leaned over to kiss her on the forehead as my tears streamed down her soft cheeks. I held her hand and thought how painful life could be.

Finally at 7 p.m., I whispered, 'Bye, Mum, I love you.' I went home and started pacing again. I knew I wouldn't sleep and decided to take one of Mum's sleeping pills. As I lay there, I was mad at God. I asked Him why He hadn't given her more time with me. It wasn't fair! As I started to drift off it was as if I heard Him say that during her last days he placed her in my hands because He knew that's where she would want to be. Then I fell into a deep sleep.

I was still going through the healing process when only five weeks later my Aunt Joyce called me to say that my real father had been sick and had just passed away.

It was good to see the end of that year. The following Christmas was lonely, but I got through it. One has no choice.

Chapter Twenty-One

Finally, it was the Spring of 1985. How good it was to see the grass turning green and the sunshine. It seems to give a person a new breath of life. I started to feel like getting away for a while. I hadn't taken a vacation in a long time so I called an old friend of mine that I had once worked with. Her name was Peggy and she lived in West Virginia. She had called me a few times in the past and had extended her invitation for me to visit her any time I wanted.

Peggy was so happy when I called her. She was suffering the pangs of loneliness since she had recently gone through a divorce. It was all set. I told her I would be arriving on the following Wednesday and she told me she would meet me at the bus station.

The first two days of my visit with her were spent sightseeing and the scenery was beautiful. I took a lot of pictures and even thought that I could live there permanently, I liked it so much. Friday night we went dancing. It was good to get out again, and Peggy told me how happy she was that I had decided to go there. We were having such a good time and found a variety of things to do. Saturday we stayed around the house and had a cook-out in her back yard. We did a whole lot of talking and just basically had fun.

★

It was Memorial Day weekend. On the Sunday we went driving around again and stopped for lunch, then went home. It was about 7 p.m. when Peggy suggested that we go for a cocktail as she didn't feel like staying home again. Peggy said there weren't too many places to go around there, but there was a place about half a mile down the road. She said she had never been there in her life because it had been known to have a very bad reputation for drugs and fights. She went on to say that she had been hearing good reports on the place for the last three months. It had gone under new management and the guy had really cleaned the place up. I said to her that we could stop in and have one and if we didn't like it we could leave. So we jumped in the car and headed down there. The name of the place was the Dog House Saloon. My first impression when we walked in was how immaculate the place was and the floor shone like glass. The only people in the place were the ones sitting at the bar. We also wanted to sit at the bar so we could rap with the people. While I stood and ordered our drinks, Peggy was looking for two seats. As the bartender handed me the drinks, Peg said, 'I guess we will have to sit at a table,' as there were no seats left at the bar. We reluctantly sat at a table in the corner and we sort of felt left out. We were sitting there having a nice quiet talk and enjoying our cocktails, when I looked toward the door, which I was facing. Two guys came banging through and the one in front had a gun. He stopped in his tracks and pointed it at the bartender. I turned to Peg and said, 'Look at that guy, he's pulling some kind of a joke with a toy gun.' At that moment he pulled the trigger and I saw the bartender grab his shoulder. Then he reached under the bar and grabbed a gun. We knew at that point that it was no joke and that something awfully wrong was happening. Peg and I went crazy. We started to push each other into the Ladies' Room, and once in there we locked the door from the inside. I remember standing there with my hands over my ears as I tried to block out the sound of gun shots. We were terrified at the thought of what we were going to see once we left the rest room, but within a matter of minutes everything went deathly silent. Someone had seen us head for the rest room and they tapped on the door and told us it was safe to come out. As we slowly walked out, cops and paramedics came walking into the bar. They asked everyone not to leave until they questioned us. I had to tell the policeman exactly what I saw, but also had to tell him that I was only visiting that area for one week, as I was on vacation. He told me not to worry.

Three people had been shot First the bartender; he had been hit in the shoulder but he was going to be all right. He shot back at the guy who had walked in with the gun, who was lying dead near the door. The third person was a poor man who had been sitting at the bar with his wife. He had been caught in the crossfire and shot in the head.

Peg and I couldn't wait to get out of that place. We just wanted to go home. The police let everyone leave about forty minutes later and Peggy kept apologising to me for taking me there. I asked her if she had ever heard of any other shootings that had taken place there. She said, 'Never!' and I told her she didn't have to apologise, that it was one of those dreadful things that a person can't predict.

Once we got inside her house, we locked all the doors. It was as if we wanted to feel safe. Needless to say it was another sleepless night for both of us. We decided to cool it for the remainder of my time there but our nerves had been a little bit shattered.

★

Finally, my vacation came to an end and I boarded the bus home. I told Peggy I would call her the following weekend. During the bus ride I thought of the nice times we had had then I thought of the shoot-out and how utterly ironic it was to think of my first impression as we walked in. It was beautiful and yet in less than one hour, three people were shot and blood spattered everywhere. I felt relieved to come home to my safe little apartment.

I called Peggy the following weekend as I promised and I asked her if she had heard any more about the bar-room incident and the reason why it had happened. She told me that the two guys that came in with the gun had been there a couple of hours earlier and started to get argumentative so the bartender had politely asked them to leave. They went drinking elsewhere and held a grudge, so they decided to return and shoot the bartender. The poor guy in the middle survived but they were unable to remove the bullet from his head. The other guy that had banged through the door had been picked up and put in jail. Peg and I decided to get off the morbid subject and at least talk about the nice times we had had. Once again we promised to keep in touch and maybe the next time she could come and visit me.

Chapter Twenty-Two

I lived on the East Coast for another four years when it got to the point that I couldn't stand the loneliness any more. Maybe it was my own fault. I was a real homebody, but did go out at weekends and I never met anyone that I wanted a relationship with.

During the year of 1989 I started to think about going back to England and possibly finding a job there, I felt I needed to be among relatives. My kids were grown-up and married and I didn't want to feel as if I was a burden to them. I started to pack my belongings bit by bit and stacking the boxes one on top of the other. I didn't put an address on them right away, just in case I changed my mind.

I sure missed my mum's letters, but always looked forward to June's. She wrote a pretty lengthy letter. It was at the time I was packing that June was writing to tell me how worried she was about her husband, Jack. His health was failing badly and he had lost an awful lot of weight. It was one Saturday afternoon when Jack himself called me. He said June was out shopping and he wanted to talk to me in private. He asked me if I would consider moving back to California. I knew what he was getting at – he was dying and wanted me to be with June. I told him he had sort of caught me off guard and I had never thought of going back there. Actually I didn't even have any desire to return to California but I did tell him I would think about it. I hung up the phone and started to wonder just what I should do. Finally I told myself, What's one more year? June was my best friend and I felt sure she was going to need me so I made my decision. I would go for twelve months, then I could go to England from there.

I was unable to leave right away. I still had more packing to do and furniture to get rid of and it was two months later before I was able to leave. Unfortunately, Jack passed away before I made it there. I felt so bad that I couldn't have seen him one more time, but at least he had peace of mind when I assured him I was going there.

Once again June and I were hugging at the airport. She was laughing and crying at the same time and I knew I had made the right decision. June was taking Jack's death pretty badly. She was renting one of the cutest little places I had ever seen. It was right in the middle of a field and the owner of the place had sheep and horses all around. It was like living on a ranch. As I looked through the window it was like a beautiful picture postcard.

The one thing that worried me was where in the world would I find a job around there as it was so country. I knew I had to make some kind of a living if I was going to be there for a year. Then I thought of Scarlett O'Hara's famous words, 'I'll think about that tomorrow.' Tomorrow came.

June said, 'Come on, I'll show you around our little community, a quaint little town called Penngrove.'

I still couldn't see anything in the way of work, so I decided to put a notice on the bulletin board at the convenience store, to do housekeeping. Sure enough I started to get phone calls and before I knew it I was working for two or three people in the area. I felt I was at least making enough to see me through. If there was one thing I couldn't stand it was to go to clean someone's home and to find they didn't have the right cleaning equipment, so I went and bought a mop; a broom; a small step ladder and a rag bag which contained everything from furniture polish to Windex. Plus half a dozen other products; and on the top I would put a plastic bag with fresh clean rags for each day.

June and I would take one day a week and just get out for the day. It seemed to be the only time that June would snap out of her terrible depression. She was a changed person once she got in the car for our day out.

I had been at June's place about three and a half months when one morning I started to think about my bosses that I used to work for, Mark and Phillip. It happened to be our day out that day, so I suggested to June that we stop by Phill's Place. I was curious to see if Phill was still there. She said sure, we could go for lunch.

We walked into the restaurant and I peeped into the kitchen. To my surprise, there was Phill, standing at the stove, stirring something in an iron skillet. I crept up behind him and wrapped my arms around his waist. For a second he went motionless, as if some strange sensation had crept over his body. Then he glanced over his shoulder and got the shock of his life. He was so excited to see me that he stopped everything and came and had coffee with us. He hadn't changed a bit; still the same ole sweet guy. Phill asked me how long I was going to stay in California and I told him the whole story. He offered me a job, but I didn't have a car so I told him I would see how things went and would get back to him. In the meantime he took down June's phone number.

I asked how Mark was. Phill told me that he had sold the other restaurant but had bought another one about an hour away. I gave Phill a kiss on the cheek as June and I prepared to leave.

It was about 2 p.m. the following afternoon when the phone rang. I couldn't believe my ears; it was Mark. He had talked to Phill and got the phone number. He said he was coming into town to take care of some business and asked if we girls would like to meet him for a drink.

I hesitated for a moment, then found myself saying, 'Sure, we will meet you at 7 p.m. at such and such a place.' I hung up the phone and found myself trembling all over again. I told myself that I didn't want to get involved and yet at the same time I couldn't wait to see him. June and I met him at 7 p.m. He also hadn't changed. He looked so young for his age and 'still as handsome. We sat and talked for about an hour then June said she had to go on an errand and asked Mark if he would mind giving me a ride home.

He said, 'Sure, no problem.'

We sat there a little longer. I couldn't believe it when he told me that he and his wife were legally separated and had been for two years. The divorce was pending. I told him I was sorry and I always felt sad when couples broke up. Finally we left and he drove me home. He leaned over and gave me a peck on the cheek and told me it was good to see me again. I said goodnight and went in the house. I lay in bed that night thinking about him. All those old feelings seemed to have crept back. I wondered if he would call me again or just what.

It was the following Friday and I was in ecstasy. Mark called and asked me if I would like to go to dinner and dancing. He picked me up that evening, and it was wonderful. As he held me in his arms on the dance floor I had to use the word ironic again as I thought to myself, 'It's been seventeen years and here we are back together.' It was like a love story.

Once again we became lovers. We were having wonderful times. Every weekend we went dancing and Sundays were special. We would go for long drives in the country and I lived for every moment that we spent together.

Finally the Christmas holidays were getting close. Mark had made reservations for New Years Eve but he wouldn't tell me where. He said it was going to be a surprise. I bought a beautiful new dress with shoes to match as I wanted to look special on that night.

In the meantime there was something that was bothering me very much. It was June. She just wasn't snapping out of her depression over Jack's death. Months had gone by and she was just as bad as when I had first gone there. I had tried so hard to cheer her up. One day when I was driving home from work, I told myself I couldn't stand it any longer. She was making me miserable. I decided that what we needed was one of those nights around the fireplace like we used to have years ago. I pulled over and went into the package store and bought a bottle of fine wine.

I went home and waited until after dinner then I put a match to the fire and poured us a glass of wine. I turned to June and said, 'If only for one night we are going to push everything from our minds. Let's just free ourselves of the things that bother us. We deserve to feel good for a change.'

It worked like a charm. Our sense of humour was at a peak. We started to see the funny side of a whole lot of things that had happened in our lives and we especially laughed about the night many years ago when June and I went to a dance. We didn't especially care for the band, so we decided to leave around 10.30 p.m. On the way out we saw this poor guy sitting on a chair in the lobby. He was as white as a sheet and perspiring profusely. We walked over to him and led him to a couch. We told him to lie down a while until he felt better. I went to the kitchen and asked for a damp cloth. As I was wiping his face and neck, June asked him in a very professional manner, 'Sir, are you taking any kind of medication?'

He nodded 'Yes,' and pointed to his shirt pocket, then June took out a pill and placed it under his tongue.

A small crowd of people had started to gather around.

As I felt the man's pulse, we heard a guy say to the people who were looking, 'Stand back, folks. The paramedics have everything under control. The man is coming around.' June and I did not dare to look at each other.

On the way out a lady asked me where we had parked the Rescue Truck and I casually told her that we happened to be off duty. Once outside, June and I roared with laughter.

June said, 'Well, at least we revived the poor bugger.'

That happened to be one of many stories we talked about around the fireplace. It turned out to be one of the most fun nights I had ever known. We laughed for five solid hours. Finally we said good night to each other and went to our rooms holding our sides.

The next day when I arrived home from work, June was out. She and her daughter came walking in about an hour later. June had awakened that morning with bad pains in her abdomen and her daughter picked her up and taken her to the Emergency Room. They couldn't find a thing wrong with her and June said she had heard that a person could bust a gut laughing, and that's what must have happened to her. From that time on she seemed much better. It was good to see a smile on her face again.

The following week I couldn't resist having another evening around the fire. Once again we reminisced about the past, but this time it was on a more serious note. June told me that she thought I had had a pretty unusual life. She asked me if I had learned anything from my many experiences.

My answer to that was, 'Boy, have I ever!' but first I want to say I have always started my day off with a prayer. I do believe it gives you strength to get through just about anything. I then proceeded to answer her question. I said, 'Yes, I have learned a lot. First of all I think back to when I was young. When a person reaches her teenage years and has been brought up in an unhappy home, at least she should ask herself a question, and that is, 'What about my parents, what kind of a background did they come from?' Maybe their upbringing hadn't been so rosy either. It doesn't put things right, but it certainly makes you have a deeper understanding and even helps you cope a little better.

'Secondly, work at your marriage more, but it takes both partners. I have regrets that my ex and I didn't try harder – the grass sure isn't always greener on the other side.

'What's important is if a divorce is inevitable and kids are involved. The one who leaves those kids should always keep in touch with them. It pays off. My kids and I are super close. Thank God, we visit each other whenever we can get the chance.

'Thirdly, and this doesn't just apply to people starting over after a broken marriage, but to anyone, be careful whom you take home. Get to know them first. Trying to help someone who has been in serious trouble doesn't always work out. You can end up having your own life shattered.' I couldn't help thinking about the horrible incident in that bar room where the shooting took place. It made me more selective in the places I chose to go and I realised that things like that were happening all too often. They were happening in restaurants; post offices; on the streets and even in the home, but it still doesn't hurt to choose a place where you think it's least likely to happen.

'Last but not least, education is very important. I am a perfect example of a person who didn't have any. Maybe I should have gone back to school when I was older, but I found I was having to work hard to survive and couldn't find the time.' I glanced over at that stupid ragbag that was sitting in the corner. I said to June, 'One of these days I am going to come home from work and throw that bloody thing in the river because, so help me God, somehow some way, I am going to reach the top!'

June leaped out of her chair, and she jumped for joy. She said, 'I love it! That's what I want to hear!'

Laughing I said, 'You sure can be dramatic!'

It was said in fun, but she sat back down and said, 'Wouldn't it be wonderful if that turns out to be a whole new experience, that one day in the future we can sit around the fireplace and talk about it!'

I said, 'It sure would.' I leaned over and put another log on the fire.

She said, 'Well, you came to stay with me for a year. I am so thankful you did and I wish you could stay for ever, but I know you have to get on with your life.' Continuing she said, 'That year will be up in a couple of months. What do you think you will do then?'

I sat quietly for a few minutes. I was thinking of Mark. We had a wonderful relationship going, but he wasn't totally free yet. I was going to have to wait and see what happened in that department.

I said, 'June, I don't want to think right now about what I will do when the year is over. I just want to think of New Year's Eve, which is only two weeks away. I don't want to look beyond that.'

I love New Year's Eve; it's my favourite night of the year. How I love the sparkle and the glitter! I want to absorb it. I want to slow dance in those wonderful arms. Mark and I will toast each other with champagne and tenderly kiss at midnight.